Paper Flow

Your ultimate guide to making paperwork easy

MaryAnne Bennie & Brigitte Hinneberg

Wrightbooks

Paper Flow Bonus
Our gift to you – the Paper Flow 28 Day Challenge

Feel like you need an extra helping hand? Most people need that extra personal touch, so we designed the Paper Flow 28 Day Challenge with you in mind! No more procrastinating, no more excuses, the challenge has it all sorted out for you. You will have a deadline, checklists and a community forum to assist you every step of the way.

Join the **Paper Flow 28 Day Challenge** today!

What is it? The **Paper Flow 28 Day Challenge** is a challenge to everybody to take a good hard look at their paperwork and to do something about it! We know it is possible to totally transform your paperwork and your life in just 28 days! We provide the structure and guidelines; you set the deadline and follow our instructions. In 28 days your paper**work** will become paper**play**!

Why do it? You will feel fantastic. You will have more energy, more time and more money. The costs of not having a paper system in place are enormous on your time, wallet, health and relationships. The **Paper Flow 28 Day Challenge** will put an end to all that and give you a brand new system that will support you forever.

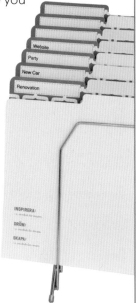

Who will benefit? Everybody will benefit from taking the *Paper Flow* challenge; households, students, executives, home based businesses, mums and dads, frequent travellers, retirees and empty nesters. Anyone who handles the paper in their life will feel supported and liberated by taking the challenge while giving their paper a total makeover.

How it works. It's really easy. All you need to do is use the *Paper Flow* system for 28 days. It starts the day you start the challenge. Simple!

**Make the decision today to let your Paper Flow.
Register to join the Challenge at**
www.paperflowbook.com

Paper
Flow

First published in 2009

This edition published in 2011 by Wrightbooks
John Wiley & Sons Australia, Ltd
42 McDougall Street, Milton Qld 4064

Office also in Melbourne

Typeset in ITC Avant Garde Gothic LT 9/16pt

© MaryAnne Bennie and Brigitte Hinneberg 2011
www.paperflowbook.com; info@paperflowbook.com

The moral rights of the authors have been asserted

National Library of Australia Cataloguing-in-Publication entry:

Author:	Bennie, MaryAnne.
Title:	Paper flow: your ultimate guide to making paperwork easy / MaryAnne Bennie, Brigitte Hinneberg.
ISBN:	9780730377030 (pbk.)
Subjects:	Paperwork (Office practice)—Management. Filing systems. Time management. Life skills.
Other authors/contributors:	
	Hinneberg, Brigitte, 1970-
Dewey number:	651.5

Cover design by Peter Reardon, Pipeline Design <www.pipelinedesign.com.au>

Internal design by Vikki Siliato, Disktress

Images supplied by kikki-K and Carla Fletcher

Printed in China by Printplus Limited

10 9 8 7 6 5 4 3 2 1

Disclaimer
The material in this publication is of the nature of general comment only, and does not represent professional advice. It is not intended to provide specific guidance for particular circumstances and it should not be relied on as the basis for any decision to take action or not take action on any matter which it covers. Readers should obtain professional advice where appropriate, before making any such decision. To the maximum extent permitted by law, the authors and publisher disclaim all responsibility and liability to any person, arising directly or indirectly from any person taking or not taking action based on the information in this publication.

Contents

About the authors

MaryAnne Bennie MaryAnne Bennie is an organising expert, speaker and director of in8 home office and life organising. As a busy working woman, with a husband, three adult children and four grandchildren, MaryAnne understands the struggle of the juggle of home, office and life. In 2002 she created the *Paper Flow* system and has since introduced thousands of people to the *Paper Flow* system through numerous  workshops and private consultations. She is a former university lecturer and holds a Bachelor of Education and a Master of Business. In order for this book to come alive, MaryAnne joined forces with author Brigitte Hinneberg and the result of their combined strengths is *Paper Flow*, the ultimate guide to making paperwork easy.

Brigitte Hinneberg is an author, presenter and business coach with a passion for helping busy people achieve work-life balance by encouraging order. Brigitte's first book, *Did You Remember The Milk?*, is the essential home organiser for very busy people. Brigitte is a certified lifestyle coach with a degree in Economics and Commerce. After a successful 12 year marketing career, Brigitte founded Momentum Coaching  and Consulting, a coaching practice helping executives and private individuals save time, money and stress. Brigitte lives in Brisbane, Australia with her husband and three children who provide plenty of inspiration for her books and organisational resources.

A word from the authors

We're all feeling the pressure to save a dollar and streamline our lives these days. But keeping on top of your current situation is near impossible if you don't have a good system in place.

Success starts with getting the small details under control. And it starts right here, right now, in your home and office.

Paper Flow works because it is a system you design for yourself. We have laid it out in a way that enables you to establish your own successful system. We give you the steps, ask you to make some choices and show you what others have done. At all times you are in the driver's seat. All the elements of a successful system are covered. You won't miss a thing.

Having an organised paper system is good for your state of mind and your bank balance. Loved ones will enjoy a less stressed you, and your colleagues will benefit from a more efficient, responsive and organised team member who's a few steps ahead of the game.

You'll love having more time to spend on your big plans, instead of sweating the small stuff.

Don't spend another moment in paper chaos: let your *Paper Flow*!

MaryAnne and Brigitte

> Go with the flow
>
> *Marcus Aurelius*

Introduction

Paper flows through our lives. It maps our journeys, showing where and when we were born, our progress through school, where we travel and where we choose to call home. Paper celebrates our life achievements through school reports, diplomas, degrees and work contracts. We accumulate permission documents such as licences, accreditations and endorsements. Marriage and birth certificates are evidence that we loved and we left living legacies. Invoices, account summaries and receipts show what we exchanged our hard-earned money for, be it electricity, lounge suites, houses or holidays.

We begin life with a single piece of paper – the birth certificate is the wellspring – and we gather more and more simply by living. At times the paper flows like a torrent, and just like any river, it is a great servant but a poor master. When the river bank breaks and paper floods our lives, all we can do is try to keep our heads above it all and hope that we don't get snagged by a lost tax receipt, misplaced warranty or unpaid insurance reminder. This can put enormous stress on relationships, as well as create serious consequences downstream.

Every person is unique, in their lifestyle, personal history, needs and goals for the future. In *Paper Flow*, we demonstrate how to create a simple, personalised system for managing the paper that flows into your home and office. We will show you how to make sure your paper buoys, rather than drowns you.

You can start to save yourself from the paper deluge by acknowledging some truths about paper:

1. Paper needs to earn the right to take up your space: Paper will fill the space made available for it. We have an infinite capacity to bring paper into our lives, but we have a finite space in which to store it. Consider your storage space when deciding what to keep. Everything in your home and office is competing for precious space, so make sure your paperwork is earning its right to be there.

2. Look after the 20 per cent: Most paper is unnecessary. Only 20 per cent of the paper we keep is ever actually referred to again. A whopping 80 per cent of it is never going to be looked at again, ever! Look after the 20 per cent you need and release the rest.

3. It's always urgent when you can't find it: When paper is needed, it's needed now! You never know when you're going to need that important document, but when you do, it's almost always in a hurry. These unexpected deadlines send you into a spin as you madly search through your paper jungle. The person who can quickly and easily find that document when they need it, wins.

4. Paper likes to be with its friends: Your paper wants to be with paper just like it. It wants to be with similar types of information and with similar shapes and sizes. When the important documents are mixed in with the 'sentimental', and the 'sentimental' is mingling too closely with the 'nice to read but not really necessary to keep', you get paper friction. When large receipts are mixed together with small dockets, neither is happy with the other's storage solution because of their different shapes and sizes. When paper is disorganised, you feel disorganised too. It's contagious.

5. Your paper will tell you how it wants to be stored: It really is that simple. Many people get sidetracked by frustrating questions, such as: Does my home insurance information get a file of its own, or should I file it under 'House'? Do management reports go under 'Company Reports' or by subject file? The possibilities seem endless. You just need to listen to your paper, it will tell you what it needs.

6. Storage is a tool, not a solution: Storage is not the answer to disorganised paperwork. Storage containers, files, and stationery are merely tools, and a tool without a system is just clutter. People buy all sorts of tools to contain their mess, only to have it add further chaos as they shift the piles into suspension files, then folders, then boxes and back to suspension files. It's like the outfit you bought in a hurry that doesn't quite fit; no matter how hard you try, it's not going to look or feel good. *Paper Flow* creates the right system which then determines your storage needs, not the other way around.

7. Paper will evolve: Your paperwork system will change and evolve, just like you. A good system will adapt, expand and contract as your needs and lifestyle change. A good paperwork system preserves your past, documents your present and anticipates your future.

8. Paper needs to flow: As it flows in, through and out of your home and office it needs a home at each stage of its journey. When paper doesn't flow, we experience 'office constipation'. When paper is allowed to flow and is in the right place at the right time you relax and feel supported. You are able to concentrate on the 'here and now', knowing that your paperwork is sorted, organised and filed.

These eight truths form the basis of the *Paper Flow* philosophy. *Paper Flow* is a fail-safe, tried and tested approach to paper management that will support you in the real world, through all the ebbs and flows of life.

How to use this book

Paper Flow provides step-by-step instructions on how to move paper in, through and out of your home and office. It will take about a week to get it up and running, and then it will take you around ten minutes a day to keep your day-to-day paperwork in check.

Keep a notebook handy as you work through the book so you can jot down any 'to dos', key decisions and any items you need to buy.

Chapters 2 to 7 take you step by step through each of the elements of your *Paper Flow* system. It is recommended that you work through each chapter sequentially so that you can immediately and continually move your paper forward, equipped with all the tips and tools you need. This will prevent you from having to backtrack.

Chapter 8 is devoted to handling any questions or issues that you may have once your paper system is up and running.

 Case studies in each chapter offer you real life examples of *Paper Flow* problems and solutions as experienced by a wide variety of people in different situations.

 Tips for success highlight for you some of the key ideas and concepts that will give you the real *Paper Flow* edge.

 Decide now! prompters will ask you to pause for a moment and make a decision. If you're not sure, rather than skipping ahead, just trust your judgement at that point in time and make a choice so you can move on to the next step of the *Paper Flow* system. Once your system is up and running you can always go back and make adjustments.

 eFlow will help you apply *Paper Flow* principles, techniques and tips to your computer files. All the information in your life regardless of whether it is paper or computer based will flow effortlessly in, through and out of your home and office.

The gallery of tools on page 159 is your ready reference guide to tools mentioned throughout the book.

Paper Flow will turn your paperwork into what you want it to be – your friend and support. You will be able to find anything you need when you need it. You will be able to easily and confidently handle all the paperwork that comes your way. And you will know exactly where to put each piece of paper without a moment of hesitation or doubt. Waste no more time, money, energy and space! Read on for a solution that streams your *Paper Flow* into a logical, low-maintenance, sustainable system.

> The truth is that our finest moments are most likely to occur when we are feeling deeply uncomfortable, unhappy, or unfulfilled. For it is only in such moments, propelled by our discomfort, that we are likely to step out of our ruts and start searching for different ways or truer answers.
>
> *M Scott Peck*

The cost of paper chaos

Maybe someone gave you this copy of *Paper Flow* because they thought you could do with a few hints? Or perhaps you were browsing in a book store and happened upon it, deciding once and for all that *Paper Flow* would finally put an end to your paper chaos? Or you may be a person who already has an organised paper system but is looking for a few extra tips and ideas. Regardless of your starting position, taking stock of the cost of paper chaos will show you the true value of creating *Paper Flow* in your home or office.

Many people are surprised to learn just how much their paper chaos is costing them. The true cost of the paper jam in our lives is enormous: we lose sleep worrying about where we put things; we spend ridiculous amounts on fines, interest and late fees, as well as repeat purchases for items we can't find; we decline invitations from friends; and we spend too much time looking for important documents. We are never in the moment – we arrive late and leave early. Our 'busyness' creates a barrier between us and the world, and we can never seem to just relax.

People often tell us they feel like a fraud when they're disorganised, that their public persona is concealing their private chaos. It's like the duck that always looks calm on the surface, but is paddling like mad underneath to stay afloat. Our confidence is eroded and we start worrying about what our friends and colleagues would think if they knew the state we were in. No wonder we wake up in the middle of the night and feel like screaming 'Enough!'

Carol counts the cost of avoiding paper

Carol moved house three times in five years. Over that time much of her paperwork remained in boxes. When Carol finally got all her paper together it completely filled a large dining room table. It stood like a volcano ready to erupt. Once she had sorted through it all, Carol discovered at least $6000 worth of unclaimed medical expenses, ten unbanked cheques amounting to $2500, $275 in cash (some still inside their birthday cards!), two passports that she had reported as lost costing her $500 to replace, unpaid bills that had attracted late fees and interest charges amounting to a whopping $5420, a gym membership that she had forgotten to cancel two years ago, so far costing $1400 and for which her account was still being direct debited, two insurance policies for the same car costing $700, and a whole swag of unused gift vouchers valued at around $2000.

Wading through her paperwork, Carol spent an enormous amount of time collating documents, making phone calls, filling in forms, paying additional fees, making appointments, attending meetings, writing letters and checking statements. It took an immense toll on her emotionally and caused friction with her partner, who had thought she was in control of their paperwork.

At her lowest point, she felt drained, defeated, frustrated, stupid, overwhelmed and angry at herself in particular, and everyone else in general. She wondered how others viewed her in her state of chaos. Despite all the clutter, she knew she was an intelligent and capable woman and all she wanted was her paperwork to reflect this. Once she conquered the paper flood she felt a new sense of confidence and calm knowing that she could handle anything that came her way. She vowed that things would never get like that again.

What is your paper chaos costing you?

Take your notebook and pen and spend a few minutes answering these questions to calculate the 'true' cost of your paper chaos.

Financial costs

How much money do you waste each **month** on the following?

- Interest, fines and charges for overdue or expired lodgements or payments
- Refund value of goods that were unable to be exchanged or returned due to lost receipts
- Paying premium prices for things left to the last minute
- The value of lost or expired gift vouchers that you can no longer redeem
- The amount of unclaimed medical, work and tax expenses
- The interest foregone on unbanked cash and cheques

Time costs

How many hours do you waste each **week** on the following?

- Looking for documents you know you have but cannot find
- Duplicating paperwork you have already partly or fully completed but cannot locate
- Sorting and re-sorting items but never really filing them away

Emotional costs

How much emotional energy do you waste each **week** on the following?

- Worrying about what lies hidden within your paper jungle
- Battling with loved ones over who's to blame
- Procrastinating about even the simplest of tasks
- Feeling disconnected from the present while you struggle with your past

Professional and social costs

How would your colleagues and friends **perceive** you on each of the following?

- Ability to meet deadlines
- Level of organisation
- Punctuality
- Capacity to follow through
- Stress levels

Personal costs

Do you answer 'yes' or 'no' to the following statements?

- Being disorganised is affecting my relationships and family
- My level of disorganisation is taking its toll on my self-esteem and confidence
- The stress of being disorganised is affecting my enjoyment of my home, my work and my life

Now calculate the true cost of your paper jam:

Step one: add up your financial costs incurred each month from the first question and multiply the result by 12.

Step two: take the total number of hours wasted each week and multiply it by 52. Now multiply that number by your hourly rate. If you don't currently work in paid employment, simply estimate how much your time would be worth per hour if you did.

Step three: add the financial and time costs together to see just how much money you are wasting each year.

Step four: list your top emotional, professional and personal costs.

Now do your own 'before and after' cost snapshot by keeping these answers in your notebook. You should re-assess your answers once you have spent three months using *Paper Flow*. This is also a good time to take a 'before' photo of your current paper situation.

Time for forgiveness

If you're feeling overwhelmed by the sheer weight of it all, we hear you and we know how you feel. By identifying the true cost of your paper chaos, you have just discovered the real worth of being organised. Just think about all the time, money, emotional energy, credibility, love, confidence and respect you're going to gain from now on! We promise that if you follow the *Paper Flow* system, you will easily manage all your day to day paper and notice life changing benefits.

Now in order to move forward, you first need to forgive. So, take a moment right now to forgive yourself for all the bills you haven't paid, the items you haven't filed, the white lies you've told, the blame you've placed on others, the arguments you've caused, the unbanked cheques and the missing important documents. Forgive yourself for every last paper crime you feel guilty or upset about.

From now on

Now you're ready to draw a line in the sand and to take a step across that line from your past chaos to a wonderful place called 'From Now On'. This place is your fresh start, which will set you up for success and support you through all the changes you will inevitably experience in your life. *Paper Flow* will set you up forever and you will never have to reinvent your paper system again. From now on you will move all paper into your new *Paper Flow* system on a regular and routine basis. It will soon become a habit requiring little thought. We have laid it out so that it is very easy to follow. As your confidence and expertise builds you can adapt and change *Paper Flow* to give it more of your own personality and style. You will wonder how you ever lived without *Paper Flow* and why you ever struggled with paperwork in the first place.

Your first task after crossing into 'From Now On' is to put a stop to your tendency to create piles because you don't want to make a decision, otherwise known as 'piling behaviour'. From now on you are not allowed to add to a pile or to start a new one. There are two ways you can do this. If you only have a few piles to deal with, place a sign on top of each of them saying 'Top of the Pile'. This sign will act as a deterrent to adding to the pile and will keep you in check. However, if you have a lot of unsorted paper all over the place, we suggest that you bundle up all your piles and place them into a neat stack of boxes. This will prevent the clutter from overwhelming you and distracting you from the job at hand. You will be dealing with the backlog soon enough but not until your system is set up and each piece of paper has a designated place to go. Once your *Paper Flow* system is set up you will then have the option of sorting out all your piles in one big job or drip feeding them into your new system a few items at a time. Whichever way you choose, those piles will disappear forever.

How life could be

Having a well organised office provides you with a solid foundation and gives you the confidence to pursue your dreams. This foundation represents your base, and from this base you can go in any direction you choose. As each opportunity comes along, you can decide with a clear head what you want to do. You are free to take on new opportunities and you know when you've got enough on your plate. Instead of always having to say 'no', you can now say 'yes' without guilt or hesitation. You get to spend time on the important things with the important people in your life, instead of running around undoing past mistakes and chasing lost time. You'll feel free and invincible knowing that you are organised and ready for anything. Now let the *Paper Flow* journey begin!

Nothing is particularly hard if you divide
it into small jobs   *Henry Ford*

Harness your incoming paper
in seconds

Have you checked the letterbox? Are there any notices in your child's school bag? Did you grab those web pages off the printer? Don't forget those glossy holiday brochures still in your briefcase. Business cards from your meeting, phone messages hastily scribbled down in your notebook, a lovely wedding invitation. All of this is incoming paper and it continually streams into our homes and offices every day.

The best place to start when creating your new *Paper Flow* system is at the beginning: dealing with the paper that has just come in. We were all promised a paperless office but it doesn't seem to be coming any time soon. Paper arrives without any effort on our part: bills, important notices and junk mail. Add to that the items we bring in of our own accord: brochures, website downloads, magazines and newspapers. No wonder we feel overwhelmed!

The incoming paper station

You are about to learn a fail-safe, pain-free solution for dealing with your

Alice's love:hate relationship with paper

Alice gets excited about new paper coming in. She routinely prints information from her computer to read and she regularly brings home information on a variety of interests. Each day she approaches her letterbox with great anticipation. She scans the contents eagerly to discover what new items await her attention. Usually it's a bill or two, maybe a few statements, brochures and junk mail, and occasionally a letter or postcard from a friend. By the time she has returned to her front door, Alice has entered the state we like to call 'mail complacency'. Losing all interest, she temporarily parks her half-opened mail on the kitchen bench or dumps it on her desk and moves on to other more pressing things. This is known as 'mail denial'. It is all downhill from then on.

The piles around Alice's house continue to fester and grow each day until a friend rings one evening to say she's coming over. Alice has three minutes to do the 'paper chase'. This is a frenzied snatching up of the various paper piles and a frantic shoving of it all into the laundry basket, the top drawer of her desk or under the bed.

About ten days later, the mail that arrives has a greater urgency; reminder notices, disconnection notices and mail advising of additional fees. Her blood pressure starts to rise and suddenly the daily trip to the mailbox is not so exciting. Because her old mail is out of sight and out of mind, finding the original notices is out of the question, it's just too hard.

Alice has committed two fatal crimes against paper: she ignored it when it arrived and she swept it under the carpet, attracting additional fees and consequences like a magnet. If only she had dealt with everything the first time, she could have saved herself a lot of time, energy and money.

incoming paper. We will show you how to create an in-tray that will suit, serve and support you. Follow these four simple steps and the job will be done.

Step 1: Choose a location

Choose a spot where you will park your incoming paper each day. Think about where your current paper piles collect and that could be the natural spot for you. Typical locations include the kitchen bench, a desk, a hall table or on a credenza. Think about the number of people using the in-tray, the layout of your home and office and personal preference. Make sure the spot is convenient to everybody who uses it.

> **!** **Where will you locate your in-tray?**

Step 2: Choose an in-tray container

The humble in-tray should never be underestimated for its impact on your *Paper Flow* system. The in-tray holds your paperwork in one location until you're ready to deal with it.

When deciding on your in-tray, consider:

- the type and size of items coming in, especially if you regularly receive large, confidential or fragile items
- the volume and number of items received daily
- the number of people who will use the in-tray
- its location and how it suits the décor

Common kinds of containers used for in-trays are the traditional flat single or tiered tray, a magazine box, pigeon holes, drop down files, a decorative platter or basket, or a box.

You can see examples of an in-tray in the Gallery of Tools on page 159.

> ❗ **Which type of in-tray is right for you? If you don't already have this in-tray, add it to your shopping list.**

Step 3: Gather your daily tools

For a user friendly incoming paper station you need to have the right tools ready for action. Here is a list of daily tools you may want to have on hand:

- paper recycling bin
- stapler
- self-inking date stamp
- highlighters & markers
- pens & pencils
- letter opener
- adhesive tape
- calculator
- ruler
- rubber bands
- scissors
- hole punch with guide
- paper clips
- eraser
- pencil sharpener
- glue stick
- sticky notes
- label maker and tape

Your daily tools need a place to live when not in use. You may already have some of these in the top drawer of your desk. Alternatively, keeping them in portable containers like a tray or a box means your system is very versatile and flexible. You can simply carry your tools to wherever you are working, at any point in time. Of course you can have multiple sets of your daily tools. You could decide to have one in the kitchen, one in the office top drawer and maybe another elsewhere. Use common sense. If you get annoyed by not having what you need at hand, set up duplicate sets or create a portable collection.

Some basic daily tools ready for action

> **!** Where will you locate your daily tools and which containers will hold them securely together?

Tips for sharpening your tools

Since you're going to be using your daily tools every day, it's a good idea to do a routine inspection to ensure they're all in good working order. There's nothing worse than picking up a pen that doesn't work or using a stapler that jams all the time. Now may be the perfect time to invest in some good quality tools.

If you keep your daily tools in a drawer, use drawer dividers to give each item a home and stop them from sliding around when you open the drawer.

Step 4: Set some in-tray ground rules

Rule 1: Give it a date

From now on develop the habit of dating every piece of paper you receive. Do this in a consistent location, like the top right-hand corner, so it will be really easy to find at any time later on. If it's an important document or something you don't want to mark, just date it on the back. Your incoming paper may or may not be dated already by the sender. If it does have a date, its location could be anywhere on the page. The date you want to remember is the date you received it. Knowing the date you received something gives you a sense of context when you go back to it. It also gives you evidence, for example in a dispute about a bill payment. If you don't have time to date individual items immediately, simply bundle your mail together, date the top item and put the bundle into your in-tray. Using a self-inking date stamp makes dating a breeze.

Tips for opening your mail and saving time downstream

When opening your mail, discard all unnecessary items into your waste paper basket immediately.

Staple multiple pages of documents together so pages don't get lost or mixed up with other pages.

Highlight or circle important information, such as deadlines, amounts, names, addresses and dates. Use a highlighter, pen or pencil. This makes important information easy to find when you come back to it.

Which day(s) will you empty your in-tray? Draw up a schedule of the week and mark the day(s). This schedule will also be used for other tasks as you continue through your *Paper Flow* journey. An example schedule has been laid out for you in Appendix 1.

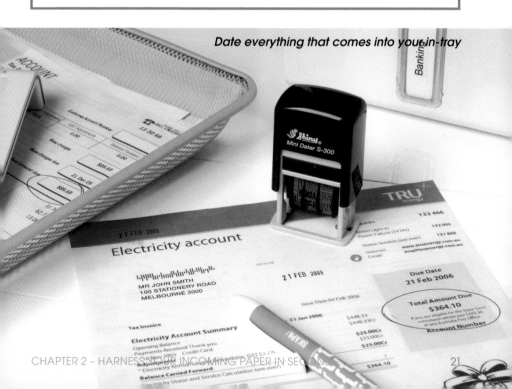

Date everything that comes into your in-tray

Rule 2: What goes in must come out

Some people think an in-tray is a place to 'keep' paper. Wrong! Have a look at yours right now. How long has your paper been hanging around in there? Days, weeks, months? Let's set the record straight, once and for all: an in-tray is a station that 'temporarily' holds paper coming into your home or office before it moves on to its appropriate destination.

For your *Paper Flow* system to work, you must commit to emptying your in-tray on a regular basis. An empty in-tray is a sign that the system is working. How often you need to empty your in-tray depends on who you are and what you do. Make sure you set a realistic goal. Daily is ideal, but for most households once or twice a week would ensure that paper keeps surging onward and outward. For businesses it may be more realistic to empty it once or even twice a day.

Tips for staying motivated

Build in a reward. Sometimes we need a little more motivation to engage with the contents of our in-trays other than the obvious reward of simply reducing the pain of the paper pile-up. We've observed that people who put a reward in the bottom of their in-tray are more likely to empty it routinely. What would put a smile on your dial when you get to the end of your paper pile? Perhaps it would be a ten-dollar note, some chocolate, an inspiring quote or a photo. Each time you completely empty your in-tray you are rewarded by what you find on the bottom of the tray.

What reward will you put at the bottom of your in-tray?

Lock in time to empty your intray

Rule 3: Always start at the top

When you empty your in-tray, start with the top item and work your way to the bottom. Starting at the bottom of your in-tray, tackling the older stuff first can lead you on a wild goose chase. For example, a reminder notice to pay an outstanding bill may have cost you a late fee. But if you were dealing with your older paper on the bottom of your in-tray first, you may see the original bill and pay it without realising you owe an extra $15. You've then under-paid the bill and now you have to double-handle it. How annoying! Likewise, an event may have been re-scheduled or moved, so now you'll be in the picture, dealing with the most up to date information first.

Rule 4: You can never go back

Just as water can only flow downstream, so too must your paper keep flowing onwards and outwards. Whenever you remove an item from the in-tray to process it, it can never go back into the in-tray, never, no matter what. Don't be tempted to put it back in, even if you don't have time to deal with it straight away. In further chapters you will see that every item from your in-tray will always have a place to go even if you can't fully deal with it right now. We don't want your in-tray to turn into the 'Too Hard Basket'. What goes in, must come out and for *Paper Flow* to work, it's a one-way street.

Tips for by-passing the in-tray

If you have the time and ability to respond to paper as soon as it arrives, date stamp it then deal with it immediately and skip the in-tray. It is still important to have your in-tray set up for those times you can't handle items immediately. Once set up, you can express past the in-tray whenever you like!

 **eFlow**

You now have a dedicated spot for all your incoming paper. On your computer, your incoming email is automatically sent to one spot, your inbox. That makes life pretty easy. You simply need to apply the same rules to emptying your email inbox as we have just shown you for your incoming paper. Choose set times during the day that you will open your emails. Start at the top and keep going until you've tackled them all. Build in a reward for finishing your emails. Once you've opened them, don't leave them in your inbox, or worse, mark them as 'unread'. The following chapters will show you how to keep your electronic 'to dos' flowing. In the meantime set up an 'in-tray'folder in your My Documents folder for any documents that you need to read or deal with later.

Stopping the inflow

To reduce the amount of incoming paper, simply prevent it from hitting your mail box in the first place. You can:

- Put a 'no junk mail' sign on your mail box
- Contact the 'do not mail' register and get your name put on it to limit direct marketing mail
- Ask to receive newsletters, statements and bills electronically where preferred
- Set up a direct debit facility for bill payments
- Stop printing off items you may never need

> **!** **Which incoming items will you put a stop to right now?**

Tips for reducing email

Reduce the number of emails coming into your inbox by unsubscribing from as many unnecessary mailing lists as possible. Also, remember that while email is a relentless stream, you need to be its master and manage the flow.

Schedule regular times for checking and responding to emails so you don't turn into an email slave. A quick phone call can often stop an entire thread of emails.

Give people a sense of how you work. Let people know when you answer your emails. Let people know how you prefer to receive information and your approximate response time. Some people are getting many hundreds of emails every day making it impossible to get any other work done at all. You need to decide how much is enough and work on email reduction on a daily basis.

Cruise control

Let's look at your results so far. You have:

- [ ] set up an in-tray at a dedicated spot to temporarily hold your incoming paper
- [ ] assembled your daily tools
- [ ] started dating everything that comes in
- [ ] scheduled regular times to completely empty your in-tray
- [ ] taken action to stop unwanted paper and emails from coming in
- [ ] begun from the top when emptying your in-tray
- [ ] set up an in-tray on your computer
- [ ] learned that once paper is removed from your in-tray, it moves out and never goes back

Further downstream

In the next chapter you will set up a system for handling all of your regular 'to do' paperwork. All paper that leaves your in-tray will make a brief stop at the 'recurring action station'. Setting up this station properly will cut down the time and energy spent on dealing with the actual tasks. You'll find your regular to-dos much easier to manage on a day to day basis. Read on, follow our instructions and let the *Paper Flow* continue.

> We are what we repeatedly do
>
> *Aristotle*

Staying on top of routine paperwork

Have you paid the telephone bill? Have you called your friend? Have you used that gift certificate you received for your birthday? Have you lodged your work expense claim? Where's the new phone number for the dentist? Nag, nag, nag. We all have items which nag us until they are done. They interrupt us at the worst of times, they make us less productive and efficient, they prevent us from sleeping soundly and they leave a trail of consequences if neglected. We have a name for these: they are called 'recurring actions'.

Your recurring actions are simply your 'to do' paperwork which needs somewhere to live until it is done as well as a nifty system for getting it done. This type of paperwork requires attention and action on a regular and routine basis. When our 'to dos' are done, we feel focussed and are liberated from that nagging voice in our heads.

We will now show you how to set up a station to sort and house your recurring action paperwork. Even with the best of intentions, you can't handle every piece of paper or task as soon as it arrives. Once your station is set up you can relax knowing exactly where each piece of paper is, and what you need to do with it next. Then we're going to show you a simple approach to getting your recurring actions done each week, in the quickest possible time.

Recurring actions are an inescapable fact of life. We are all in the same boat when it comes to these guys, regardless of who we are or what we do for a living. Once you set up your recurring action files, they will be set up forever. We like to think of them as our 'forever' files.

The recurring action station

Setting up your recurring action station is easy and takes six simple steps.

Step 1 Decide what you need

Think about the kind of recurring actions that hit your in-tray on a regular basis. You will probably recognise most of them on the list below:

Most people need:

- *'Bills to Pay'* for bills or statements that need paying
- *'Contacts to Enter'* for names, addresses, emails, phone numbers, birthday details, business cards and website addresses you need to enter into your electronic or paper-based address book
- *'Claims to Make'* for medical and insurance claims, prescriptions, gift vouchers, tickets, accepted invitations and notes regarding lent or borrowed items like books, money and CDs
- *'Correspondence to Complete'* for letters, emails, phone calls, items pending or awaiting a response and invitations needing a reply
- *'Items to Read'* for books, articles, reports, brochures, letters and newsletters you wish to read
- *'Items for Other People to Action'* for employees, associates and family members' attention
- *'Items to File'* for items that require no further action other than filing

Setting up your recurring action files

Can you ever imagine a time when you won't get bills to pay, contacts to enter, claims to make, correspondence to complete, items to read or items to file? We can't imagine that day either. So you can see why we call these 'forever' files: they will serve you forever.

In addition to the above, if you run a business you may need some or all of the following:

- 'Website to Update' for content changes and ideas
- 'Payments/Receipts to Process' for all the completed transactions which need to be entered in your accounting system such as invoices, purchases, expenses, wages and remittance advices, once the transactions have been made

- *'Invoices to Create'* for all receipts, expenses and timesheets relating to each client or job awaiting invoicing
- *'Sales Leads to Follow Up'* for prospects, referrals and people or businesses to contact
- *'Database to Update'* for adding, deleting or changing customer and prospect contact details
- *'Purchases to Make'* for stock and supply orders
- *'Returns to Claim'* for exchanges, returns, credits, refunds

> **Which recurring action files will you need? Make a list of them now.**

Step 2 Choose a container and a location

Choose which containers are right for you, based on your personal taste, budget and the number of files you need. Manila folders work very well for recurring actions. The front section of filing drawers, desk top files, step files and drop down files are all great containers for your recurring action paperwork. You can locate your files on your desk in a study, on your kitchen bench or on a bookcase shelf. The key is to have these files close at hand.

For filing options, refer to the Gallery of Tools on page 159 keeping in mind that successful recurring action files:

- are easily accessed and located close at hand
- allow items to be added and removed effortlessly
- are clearly distinguished from other types of files, usually by colour or style (refer to the 'Meanings of Colours' in Appendix 2 on page 149 to help you decide)
- may contain sub-files for better management of items within the file
- are portable, to allow you to work on them on the run if necessary

Tip for adding sub-files to manila folders ✓

Sometimes you will want to add additional sub-files to your recurring action files. You can do this by adding tabbed plastic pockets. For example you may like to use a five tab pocket for your 'Claims to Make' file and label the tabs: Medical Claims, Prescriptions, Tickets, Vouchers and Invitations. This makes for easier access and processing. See photo or go to Gallery of Tools on page 159 for ideas.

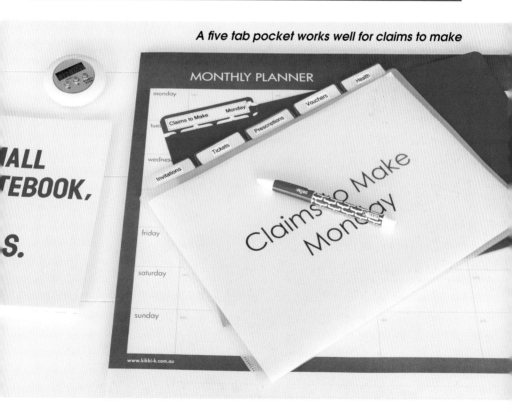

A five tab pocket works well for claims to make

Step 3 Name your files

Recurring action file names should be bossy. This should call you to action and clearly spell out what the action is. They should contain a noun and a verb, and sound commanding. Names are written in Title Case, which has a capital for the first letter of every major word in the title, as in 'Bills to Pay'. Feel free to change our suggested names to your own words but we recommend the names you choose meet the noun, verb, commanding voice and title case criteria. It really works – you'll see.

> **What names will you give your files? Write them down now.**

Items to file is a very dangerous file. So create a warning label and lock it up.

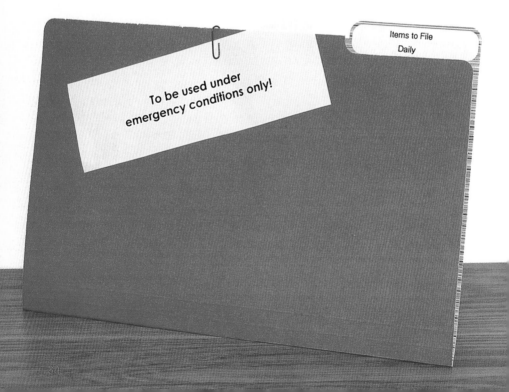

Step 4 Put it in your diary

Remember these files are the naggers in your life and the quicker they get done, the less they will nag and the less stressed you will be. You already know the longer you leave a piece of paper before you act on it, the more effort and time it takes to deal with it. At a minimum, attend to each recurring action file at least weekly. Once set up, the average household needs less than ten minutes a week to attend to each recurring action file.

Draw up a table like the one below to schedule the days you will action each of your files. The frequency you choose will depend on the amount of paperwork you accumulate on a weekly basis and how urgent your needs are. You can adjust and change the frequency to suit your lifestyle. At the end of this exercise you will have a 'Recurring Action' schedule to guide you each week. You should also make a note of the day(s) on the label of your actual file. For example your file tab will now say 'Bills to Pay – Tuesday'.

Recurring Action	Mon	Tues	Wed	Thurs	Fri	Sat	Sun
Empty in-tray	X		X		X		
Bills to Pay		X					
Contacts to Update			X				
Claims to Make					X		
Items to File	X		X		X		

Example weekly Recurring Action schedule

> **How frequently and on which day(s) will you action each file?**

Tips for finishing your filing

'Items to File' is often a problem file, tending to quickly fill beyond capacity if allowed to grow. Why not add a sign to this file saying 'to be used under emergency conditions only!' Then, bypass this file as often as possible by filing everything as you go.

For extra reinforcement try placing a paper clip on the open side of your file, creating a lock effect. You need to unlock the file in order to use it, thereby reminding yourself that this is a dangerous file, to be used with caution.

Step 5 Create your labels

Label each file with its name and the day(s) it will be actioned. Consider using a label maker. Typed and printed labels create a sense of permanency. They are visually uniform and easier for you and others to read. If you choose to hand write your labels, print clearly using dark ink. If you do them all at once you will achieve more consistency in your writing style.

Step 6 Bring it all together

Now that you have set up your files you can place each of them into its container at your chosen location.

On page 38 you see recurring action files housed in a step file on a desk.

Let's now follow the process of how paper flows from your in-tray into your recurring action station. As you take each paper item from the top of your in-tray, you need to ask it one simple question: 'What is the very next thing I need to do with you?'

The table at right shows a range of typical incoming items, a response to this question and the recurring action file into which it would go until it is actioned.

Adopting this process is critical to your *Paper Flow*. Read through the table carefully, asking the same question of each item listed. Our aim is to have you talking to each piece of paper, listening to what it has to say and filing it accordingly. Then, when you need to locate any item within your files, just ask yourself the same question again 'What is the very next thing I need to do with you?' and you will know exactly where to find it.

Incoming Item	What is the very next thing I need to do with you?	Recurring Action File
Electricity bill	Pay it	Bills to Pay
Dentist receipt	Claim against health fund	Claims to Make
Wedding invitation	Reply by post, phone or email	Correspondence to Complete
Massage gift voucher expiring in a month	Book massage appointment	Correspondence to Complete
Plumber's business card	Enter into address book	Contacts to Update
Concert ticket for next month	Take it to concert	Claims to Make
Medical test results	File it	Items to File
Telephone bill with an incorrect charge	Call phone company	Correspondence to Complete
Letter from a friend	Read and reply	Correspondence to Complete
School permission slip	Complete the slip	Correspondence to Complete
Dividend statement for Jack, another household member	Give it to Jack	Items for Jack or into Jack's in-tray
Club application form	Complete the form and post it	Correspondence to Complete
Timesheets for clients	Charge the client	Invoices to Create
Bank statement	File it	Items to File

Recurring Action File suggestions

Of course many of the items listed above can be actioned immediately, which is exactly what you should do if you can. But if you can't complete the task straight away it must go to the relevant recurring action file for you to action later.

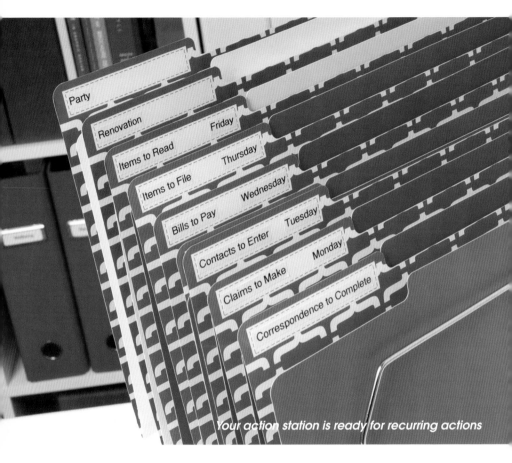

Your action station is ready for recurring actions

Rules for managing your recurring actions

Your success in keeping on top of your recurring actions depends on how well you manage and maintain their flow. By following your schedule and establishing a few simple routines you will sail through your week with a smile not a pile. Here are some tried and tested rules and guidelines to keep you in check:

- Stick to your minimum requirement of actioning each file at least weekly
- Review and increase or decrease this frequency as circumstances demand
- If you miss a date with your recurring action files, make it up at the earliest possible opportunity
- Avoid setting up too many files, instead, increase the items that go into the file by broadening your definition of what each contains
- When paying your bills write all payment details on the bill including date paid, account used, amount paid and receipt or cheque number
- When handling correspondence, make a note on the paper with the date you responded and any follow-up actions

Set some rules for each file to guide you. See how Amanda rules her files in the case study below.

Amanda rules her files

Amanda attends to her bills every Monday and she uses a 14 day rule to guide her. She opens her Bills to Pay file and asks every bill the following question: 'Do you need to be paid within 14 days, yes or no?' She pays the ones that say 'yes' and she leaves the ones that say 'no' in the file for the following week. Her rule for medical claims is to allow them to amount to over $100 before she processes a claim. If they are under $100 she lets them wait in the Claims to Make file until a few more medical bills accumulate. Prescriptions, vouchers and tickets in her Claims to Make file are reviewed weekly and claimed or processed as necessary.

What rules do you need to create to manage your recurring action files? The clearer the rules and guidelines, the easier they will be to manage and maintain.

Tip for relaxed reading

Items to Read can frequently get out of hand. With all the other things going on in your life, reading is often a low priority and can be neglected. Create a reading bag instead of a file and once a week take your reading bag filled with the week's reading, a notepad, sticky notes and a pen to a café. Spend an hour or so going through your reading and enjoy a change of environment at the same time. Your reading bag can also go with you in the car or while travelling to take advantage of any free time as it arises.

Reading material ready to take to local cafe

ⓔ Synchronising recurring actions on email

For many of us, a large volume of our recurring action paperwork arrives in electronic form. The in-box in our email program makes life easy for us by being able to display incoming emails in date order, with the most recent on top.

Just as you set up recurring action files for your physical paperwork, your email recurring actions need temporary homes as well. Your email inbox can be set up to hold your recurring actions in folders, according to what needs to happen to them next. Give them the same names as your physical files, for example, 'Bills to Pay', 'Correspondence to Complete' and 'Invoices to Create'. From now on when email comes in you simply ask it the same question you ask of your paper: 'What is the very next thing I need to do with you?' If it is a bill to be paid, place it in your electronic 'Bills to Pay' folder just as you did with your paper bills. Creating a mirror set of electronic files to reflect your new *Paper Fow* system will make life really easy for you. Once again you may bypass the recurring action files and deal with items as soon as you receive them. Set up calendar reminders to handle recurring actions in your inbox.

The 'Out Bag'

Have you ever been at the pharmacy without your prescription, at the doctor without your referral, at the accountant without that receipt, or at the post office without the item needing to be posted? Join the 'not-quite-out' club, whose membership includes the many people who have problems with the 'out' department of their recurring paper system.

When you place items into handbags and briefcases they often become lost among the myriad other items held in these places. Paper items get crushed, dog-eared, damaged or forgotten – often to be found again a few days too late.

The 'out-bag' is the best answer to moving paper from your home and office to various locations and back again. Choose a bag that's big enough to hold the sorts of paper that you need to regularly move out. Never use this bag for other things, like shopping, as its meaning will become blurred to you.

The sorts of things you would place in your out-bag include your recurring actions that now need to exit your system and make their way to:

- the bank – deposit slips, cheques, cash, forms
- appointments – documents, forms, information
- shops – receipts, coupons, vouchers
- the pharmacy – prescriptions
- insurance companies – claims for health expenses

Your out-bag could live on a hook behind a door. As soon as something needs to leave the house or office pop it into the out-bag. Then put the bag onto the front door knob, ready to go with you when you leave the house. Once in your car or over your shoulder, you'll remember what to do with the documents you've put in the bag.

You could use different out-bags for specific purposes. For example, if you are a committee member, why not keep all your things in your 'Committee Bag' ready to go to your meetings? You could even use a special compartment in your children's schoolbags for notes to and from their school. Just call it their 'Special Notes Pocket' and use it only for this purpose. Lots of people already use 'Library Bags' as out-bags. The important factors here are naming and consistency. That way you'll get used to it and it will become an indispensible part of your system.

Cruise control

Let's look at your results for this chapter. You have:

- ☐ chosen which recurring action files you need
- ☐ set up your recurring action files and placed them in their container
- ☐ named and labelled your files
- ☐ scheduled times to attend to each file
- ☐ set up appropriate recurring action folders on your computer
- ☐ dedicated an out-tray or a bag as your 'out-bag' to ensure all action items get to the right place

Your new recurring action station will serve you reliably and forever. You will always have somewhere to put items awaiting your attention, you will know where everything is at any given time and each file will only take a few minutes at a time to process.

Further downstream

Now that you've set up a system for handling your most pressing paperwork, it's time to set up an easy system for managing the projects in your life. In the next chapter you will learn how to create, advance and complete your projects, so that you are ahead of your game at work and at home. With the naggers out of the way the path ahead will be smooth.

What would you attempt to do if you knew you could not fail?

Dr Robert Schuller

Power through your projects

Wouldn't it be wonderful if you had a paperwork system that travelled the entire journey: from conceiving the great idea to delivering the project? A system that held all relevant paperwork, travelled with you when necessary and kept you on track and moving ahead until you experienced that fantastic "I did it" feeling.

Adam is about to embark on a home renovation and is gathering quotes, ideas and plans. It's time for Sonia to buy a new car and she is investigating makes and models on the internet, scanning and clipping newspapers as well as collecting brochures from car showrooms. Kim is planning a career change and is exploring further education options. Jillian and Tony are hosting Christmas at their place this year and are busy making lists and gathering ideas from magazines. What's their one common denominator? They're all working on a 'Project'. The projects in our lives can be large or small, big budget or inexpensive, work related or personal.

Unlike the never ending recurring actions that we dealt with in the last chapter, all projects have a beginning, a number of steps in the middle and an end. Projects in full flight tend to attract a lot of paper, which is added to, updated and referred to regularly. Creating, organising and maintaining your project files will keep you focussed and save you time.

This chapter will show you how to set up an organised home for any project you are working on. We'll show you how to keep your projects moving and manage the paper as your projects grow. Finally, we will show you how to dismantle your project file as each project is completed.

Identifying your key projects

The first thing to do when setting up your project files is to make a list of projects you have on the go. You might even want to separate the list into personal projects and work projects. Here are some examples:

Typical personal projects include:

- events and occasions: weddings, parties, launches
- school projects: essays, reports, research assignments
- leisure: planning holidays, new hobbies, recreational activities
- finance: loans, budgets, investing, tax returns
- career: job hunting, short courses
- home: house hunting, renovations, gardening, garage sale
- personal interests: art and craft, personal development

Typical business projects include:

- new clients or jobs
- website launches or upgrades
- seminars and events
- marketing campaigns
- cost reviews
- investment initiatives
- performance reviews
- new technology upgrades

Projects are specific in nature and often differ from each other. Three things all projects have in common are:

1. They are time-bound and they usually have a deadline
2. They require action to complete and deliver
3. Once delivered they cease to exist as projects

> **What is your current list of projects?**

Helen's hard work holiday

Helen and Alex caught up for a drink one night after work and decided to take a holiday to a tropical destination. As they chatted, Helen jotted down a couple of notes on the back of a napkin. Over the following weeks, she enthusiastically downloaded holiday options from various websites, visited the travel agent and picked up a handful of brochures, rang friends for advice and wrote down more ideas in a notebook. She gathered information like mad. Her home office started looking like a bomb had hit it, with piles of holiday paperwork strewn everywhere. Helen started to feel a bit overwhelmed by it all. There were so many brochures, she couldn't quickly locate the ones she wanted to show Alex. Nor could she find the quote from the travel agent – she couldn't even remember if it was in her notebook or on her computer. Rummaging through some piles, she noticed she had printed off the same document three times with the intention of reading it later. Her holiday started to become a pain instead of a pleasure to plan. With the deadline for paying the airfare fast approaching, Helen became stressed because she couldn't find her important information.

Helen could have saved herself a whole lot of stress and time if she'd set up a file as soon as her 'tropical holiday' idea turned into a more serious plan. Recognising that you have started a project and then setting it up properly is the key to saving a great deal of time and energy.

The good news for you, and Helen, is that there is a simple, stress-free way to set up a project file for every project you start.

Setting up the project file

Even though most projects you begin will be different from the last, it is advisable to start each one the same way. It's unlikely you will be able to anticipate every kind of paper (and how much) your project is going to attract at the outset, so it is best to grow and develop your file as the project progresses and as the need arises. Follow these simple steps to set up your project files:

1. **Choose a colour.** Start with a set of manila folders in a colour that is different from your recurring action files. From now on you'll instantly recognise a project file from a recurring action file by its colour. Again, the 'Meanings of colours' in Appendix 2 on page 149 will help you decide.

> ! **What colour will you choose?**

2. **Label your file and give it a home.** For each project you start, simply label a manila folder with the project's name and place this folder into a step file, a filing cabinet drawer or a desk-topper. See gallery of tools on page 159.

> ! **Where will you keep your 'Project' files?**

Project files ready and waiting for action

3. **eFlow: mirror your projects on your computer.** Many of your projects will also have electronic information. To help you stay consistent with your computer files, create a folder called 'Projects' on your computer. Inside your projects folder, create folders with the same names you have chosen for your paper based projects. You will immediately know where to go when looking for any project related information.

4. **Bring in the information.** Place any of your initial ideas, notes, printouts, emails, clippings, catalogues and brochures into your project files. Some items will go into your electronic folders and some will go into your physical folders depending on your preference. As long as you have matching names for your folders you will be able to easily locate anything to do with your project.

5. **Stay flexible.** As your project file grows your file storage may need to change. Don't let the folder get over-stuffed and useless. Instead, expand your mix of storage items according to your needs. For example a renovation file may include one or more manila folders for the master plan and key documents, a lever arch file for all the expenses and purchases, a magazine box for all the inspirational magazines and product catalogues, a box for samples of fabrics, tiles and colour swatches as well as a poster holder for the architect's plans. Business cards relating to that project could be stored in a plastic business card sleeve inside the project folder, or electronically on your contact system on your computer. The possibilities are endless, just do what works for you.

6. **Give it a plan.** You may like to create a planning sheet in the front of your project file with some key information about your project. This is a great timesaving tool. Every time you open the file, you will immediately see where you are up to with your project and you can proceed with the next step. Include information about the project's goal, start and end dates, budget, milestones and resources. See page 51 for an example of a project planning sheet.

Creating project flow – moving the project along

In order for projects to progress smoothly towards completion you need to keep your paper flowing. Here are a few techniques that will help:

Project paperwork comes in through your in-tray

Process your project paperwork just like all other paperwork. Projects usually require a range of different actions – there might be calls to make, bills to pay, work to complete. Paperwork for each of these activities should temporarily be held in the appropriate recurring action files until each process is completed. For example, the deposit bill from the wedding caterers comes into the in-tray, where it is then transferred to the Bills to Pay

PROJECT PLANNING SHEET

Project name:	Home renovations		
Project goal:	Build three new rooms and swimming pool by Christmas		
Start date:	Jan 2012	Finish date:	Nov 2012

Budget: $150,000

Resources needed: (people, money, information etc.)

People:

    Builder

    Architect

    Swimming Pool Design Person

Financial:

    Bank Loan

    Accountant

Information:

    Friends' contacts

    Renovating websites, etc

Key contacts:

Name	Phone	Email
Gary Smith	12345678	gsmith@email.com
Etc		

Milestone 1	Rough plans to brief architect	Complete by	
Milestone 2	Architect plans approved by council	Complete by	
Milestone 3	Secure a builder	Complete by	
Milestone 4	Commence work	Complete by	
Milestone 5	Lockup	Complete by	
Etc	Etc		

Project completion date:
(to be filled in once completed)

Comments:

This home renovation project planner provides all the important information at a glance

file. Once it is paid, it can go into the project file with all the other wedding-related costs. By placing items into your recurring action files you can be confident they will get actioned along with all your other items on a regular basis.

Schedule times and key actions into your diary

This is critical to make sure you meet your project deadlines. You can only complete your projects by investing time in them. Add key milestones as well as thinking/planning time into your diary. Some people benefit from allocating regular timeslots every week as project time. The more projects you have the more time you need to allow.

Set a limit on the number of projects you undertake at any one time

This will help you to avoid project overload. That number should be dictated by how many hours you work and how much free time you have. If you find yourself overloaded with work projects, negotiate some assistance, say 'no' to further requests and prioritise the projects you currently have.

Keep the end in sight

To keep motivated, it's important to be able to visualise the end goal. Putting a picture of the end result in the front of your file can be a fantastic way to keep motivated. For example, you could place a picture of your dream home inside the front of your renovation file to keep your motivation and vision alive through the setbacks and delays that often come with renovation projects.

Tell others about your project and its completion date

When others are involved you are more likely to stay committed and accountable for following through.

Work with others

Surround yourself with people who support and encourage you to keep your project on track. Develop a list of 'go to' people to whom you can turn for help and advice and stick that list in the front of each project file.

Mission accomplished

Once your project is complete you can enjoy the great feeling that goes hand in hand with finishing something you started. But before you move on to the next exciting project in your life, a little bit of housekeeping will help you avoid irrelevant piles building up in your office or home and ensure you don't lose important information for the future.

Now is the time to empty your project file. A lot of the information you gathered for the project will no longer be of use. For example, if your project was buying a new car, and you won't be buying another one in the near future, many items you collected can be thrown away. However, some of the paper you collected will be important to keep, such as the final purchase receipt, the dealership contact details, and the new owner's manual. Items that you keep will flow into your reference or archive files depending on what they are and how often they will be accessed. We will be addressing these in the next few chapters.

What about all those great ideas?

All projects initially start as ideas, but not all ideas turn into projects. Everybody has thoughts, dreams and ideas they may not necessarily want to action immediately. We recommend you start a dedicated project ideas book to record all of your potential ideas in the one spot. Then, when you want to go back to that idea, you will know exactly where to find your initial notes and thoughts. When creating your project ideas book, leave the first couple of pages blank and turn them into a table of contents (see the example on page 54). When you next get an idea you want to keep, give it a title and write the title and your notes on the next available right-hand page. Now all you need to do is number the page and note details on your table of contents for easy reference. When one of your ideas progresses to a project it will be easy to tear this page out to add it to your project file.

Here is an example of a project ideas book table of contents

Project ideas	Page
Business idea: building my client base	1 & 8
Business idea: creating a website	2
Photo ideas: for my albums	3
Places I want to go to before I die	4
Restaurant business names brainstorm	5
Courses I would like to investigate for next year	6
Renovation ideas: ways to improve the bedrooms	7
Building my client base through networking	8 & 1

Tips for those 'recurring' projects

Tax time comes around every year but many people don't have a routine system for handling it. Try treating your tax return as a project and you might find it easier to manage. Set up a file called 'tax return (year)' and create a project planning sheet – listing the deadline, key contacts, and a checklist of items needing inclusion in your return. Then as you gather all of your information for your tax return, put it in this file. Once the return is lodged, and your project is complete you can file all the important reference documents in a reference binder for a year or so before archiving them for as long as required.

Tips for juggling numerous projects

If you are regularly working on different projects, create a set of project files and number them Project 1, Project 2 and so on. You can then keep these files permanently set up and re-use the folders over and over again. All you need to do is keep a master list of the project names and corresponding file numbers in your ready reference file. One month, Project 3 could be a birthday party, while the following month Project 3 becomes the garden overhaul. As the project file contents change, simply update your master list.

Numbered project files stand in a row in yellow

Cruise control

Let's look at your results for this chapter. Now you:

- [ ] can differentiate between recurring action paper and project paper
- [ ] know how to set up a project file and how to label it
- [ ] understand that project paperwork will grow and contract at varying times, and that storage needs to adapt to the nature and quantity of paperwork generated
- [ ] have set up a Projects folder on your computer to house all your electronic project information
- [ ] regularly schedule time to move projects forward
- [ ] have a project or ideas book to capture ideas that may one day turn into projects
- [ ] appreciate that once a project is over it requires culling and filing and the project file ceases to exist

Further downstream

With the recurring action files and the project files explained, you are now equipped to handle any paper requiring your action with ease. In the next chapter, you will learn how to set up files to handle all the paper that you need or simply want to refer to in future. We call this Reference paper. Much of your old project information may well end up in one of these, so read on and let your paper flow!

> Success seems to be largely a matter
> of hanging on after others have let go.

William Feather

Find it when you need it

'Where should I keep my bank statements? How long do I need to keep my tax records? I put my passport in a safe place, but can't remember where it is. School reports, medical details, car registration, investments, paper, paper, paper, it's all coming at me. I'm never sure what to keep and where to keep it. I just want a filing system that works for me instead of tripping me up. I want to be able to file it all away easily and then be able to find it again quickly. Is that too much to ask?'

If this sounds like you, then relax! The answers to your paper filing issues are all here. So far we have shown you how to manage the paper that requires your action in some form. But what do you do with all the paper once you've finished acting on it? Some of it can be thrown away, hooray! But you may want or need to keep some of it.

We're now going to show you some easy, intuitive ways to store all the different kinds of paper that you want to keep handy. We call paper that requires no further action other than filing 'Reference' paper. It needs a more permanent home than your action paper. And this is where some of your action paper will end up – in a Reference file.

This is an exciting stage of establishing your new paper system because it's a one-off set-up project with big dividends. You're going to give all your 'keep-worthy' paper a visually appealing, permanent home, filed in a way that makes perfect sense to you. You will be able to retrieve any piece of paper within seconds, no matter how long it has been since you last looked at it.

Why do you keep reference paper?

People keep reference paper for a variety of reasons, the most common of which are for reflection and projection. You may want to reflect on the past to see where you have been and to project into the future to anticipate where you are going. Records from the past allow you to plan for the future.

For instance, if you hold on to your household receipts you can calculate how much you spent on running your household and use it as a basis to estimate how much you will spend in the coming year. This information is very useful if budgets are important to you or if your financial position is about to change.

Everyone feels good about having a certain amount of information, however the amount varies dramatically from person to person. How much reference paper you keep depends on your comfort level. If you are the cautious type you will most likely keep more than someone who is less cautious.

We'll take you through a simple way to create a reference system that feels comfortable and right for you. Just as you set up homes for your action paper you need to set up homes for your reference paper.

Before you get started there are three important terms used throughout this chapter:

Item – a single piece of reference paper. For example a gas bill, a bank statement, a medical report or a tax assessment notice are all items.

Category – a group of reference items that you believe go together. For example your banking category could hold bank, credit card and superannuation statements.

File – a container that holds one or more categories.

Common reference categories

Let's take a look at a list of some reference categories that are common to most people. We have kept this list as general as possible – you probably won't need them all, but it's good to have a list to work from as a starting point. Use it as a guide to design your system on a sheet of paper before you get into sorting your backlog of piles. Simply write each category heading down and list all the category items that relate to your own circumstances and lifestyle. If you have categories or items not listed here, simply add them to your list. Aim for big fat categories that capture a whole selection of items easily. Too many small categories will complicate your life. Ask this question of every item you have: 'what is the biggest, fattest category you fit into?'

- *Ready-reference information* – emergency and local area contacts, checklists, timetables, passwords and personal identification numbers (PINs) for non-financial information, instructions or procedures you regularly need, takeaway menus, filing indexes etc. Only include items you want to have at your fingertips most of the time.

- *Important documents* – birth and marriage certificates, wills, religious certificates, divorce papers, custody documents, passports, citizenship papers, organ donor registrations etc.

- *Banking, finance, investments* – bank account, department store and credit card statements, mortgage and loan statements, share certificates and dividend statements, superannuation etc.

- *Household expenses and utilities* – gas, electricity, rates, water, telephone, internet, insurance valuations, rent, maintenance and services etc.

- *Vehicle information* – registration, insurance, servicing and repairs, tolls, purchase documents, fines, parking permits, licence renewals, roadside assistance memberships etc.

- *Health* – receipts from doctors, dentists and chemists, health history, health insurance information, vaccination records, vet receipts, pet records etc.

- *Tax* – group certificates, tax assessment notices, tax deductible receipts, income receipts etc.

- *Clubs and memberships* – gym memberships, sporting clubs, professional associations, social clubs, hobby groups, classes, loyalty programs etc.

- *Education qualifications* – academic records, school reports, results transcripts, certificates, awards etc.

- *Work or career* – résumés, employment records, job descriptions, contracts, references, military service records etc.

- *Children's information* – school fees, extracurricular activities, child minding, camps etc.

- *Warranties and manuals* – warranties, manuals, instructions etc.

- *Small receipts* – any little receipts that are needed for tax purposes or future reference. For example: receipts for purchases, bill payments, petrol, parking etc.

- *Contacts* – business cards, names, addresses, phone numbers, website addresses, email addresses, birthdays, anniversaries etc.

- *Hobbies and interests* – self development, photography, cooking, fashion, diet and exercise, courses and workshops, inspiration, quotes, jokes, travel, sports, gardening, clippings, notes, scribblings, diaries and notebooks.

If you run a business, you may need a few extra categories in your reference system.

- *Supplier information* – catalogues, pricelists, trading terms and conditions, contracts etc.

- *Product and pricing information* – product specifications, descriptions, price lists, discounts policy etc.

- *Purchase information* – stock, supplies, equipment etc.

- *Customer information* – files, records, job history, specifications, plans, notes etc.

- *Sales information* – copies of invoices, cash register rolls, receipt books etc.

- *Staff information* – payroll, insurance, timesheets, travel logs, expense reimbursements, training etc.

- *Business set-up information* – registrations, certificates, permits, completed forms etc.

- *Procedures for your business* – checklists, instructions, forms etc.

Common reference files

Before you go into a panic attack thinking you need an office full of files, rest assured that most households only need about three to six lever arch folders or one filing drawer to hold most of their core reference files. Many of the categories listed may be quite small. Combining these small categories into one file minimises the number of files required. For example you may combine banking with investments if you only have a few accounts in each. However, if you have ten bank accounts then banking would need a file of its own. Common sense will guide you.

Now that you have a general understanding of what reference file categories you have, we are going to show you how to set them up.

Power sorting and big fat categories

The next step to setting up your reference files is to sort your paper into categories. Most of you will be sorting from over-stuffed files or unsorted piles. Consolidating your piles into categories will give you a clear picture of the types and quantities of paperwork you actually have.

If you are not in a position to sort your piles out right now, read on anyway. You can still set up empty reference files ready for your paperwork and you can tackle your unsorted piles a few pieces of paper at a time. Just sneak them in through your in-tray and pretend they just came in! Either way your paper will be sorted and will have somewhere to go.

The choice is yours; sort it all in one big hit or drip feed your piles into your in-tray. We recommend biting the bullet and ridding yourself of your piles forever as quickly as possible. We want you to experience that wonderful feeling of having your paperwork finally working with you and for you instead of getting you down.

Turning piles into smiles

Samantha has tried sorting out her piles a few times, but she has always ended up back where she started – Pilesville! She grabs a pile and takes it to the empty table in her kitchen. She lays out sections of her big pile into little piles on the table using sticky notes to keep her on track. She always runs out of space and has to move to her kitchen bench and along the sofa in her family room. Predictably, when it comes time for dinner, and the whole family is clambering around, Samantha reluctantly packs all her little piles back into the big pile she started with. All her energy, time and good intentions were wasted!

After attending a *Paper Flow* workshop, Samantha's pile sorting became a breeze. She learned that by sorting vertically rather than horizontally, her piles took up a fraction of the space. Vertical sorting meant that Samantha stood the items to be sorted in magazine boxes or step files – anything that kept them upright rather than spread out on the table. This kept everything in their pre-sorted categories, so Samantha was free to start and stop at any time as her family came and went, and her paper stayed vertical, taking up little room whilst awaiting completion. By saving so much time and space Samantha powered through her sorting in no time!

If you, like Samantha, have tried sorting big piles into little piles, please promise never to do it again. Instead, save time, energy and your sanity by sorting vertically from now on.

Start the power sorting process by 'setting up' for the job. A messy, cluttered environment makes it twice as hard, so find a clear space.

You will need:

- 10–20 vertical containers – magazine boxes are ideal but manila folders will work too. Place manila folders in step files or in suspension files in an empty filing drawer

- sticky notes for labels on the front of your vertical containers
- marker pens for labelling your sticky notes
- beverages to stop you going to the fridge and getting distracted on the way
- music to keep the pace up and to remove distractions
- a positive frame of mind – remember, this is going to be the very last time you ever sort a pile again!

Here's how to sort your files vertically using magazine boxes:

1. First take your magazine boxes and line them up on any flat surface. Moving some of your books from a bookshelf for a few days will give you a good sorting station. Next, bring in a chunk of paper from your unsorted piles and begin to sort, one piece at a time. Just ask each item of paper what it is and listen to its reply. If it answers 'I'm a bank statement', it goes into banking and finance.

2. Label one of your boxes 'Banking and Finance' and pop the statement into it. All other paper relating to banking and finance also goes into that magazine box in no particular order because you are just grouping your paper into 'big fat categories' at this stage.

3. The next piece of paper might be a health report. Label a box 'Health' and use it for all health-related items, again in no particular order. You now encounter a birth certificate, which goes into the 'Important Documents' magazine box, along with any other important documents you discover along the way.

4. A few unpaid bills come next, which you just pop into your existing 'Bills to Pay' recurring action file.

5. If there are magazines, create a category called 'Magazines' and place all magazines in there, regardless of what they are. When a box fills, simply create another one until all your piles are whittled down into big fat categories in their magazine boxes.

Remember: don't engage with the document you're sorting other than identifying it. Do not fall into the trap of reminiscing over the time when you had more money in the bank as you're sorting a bank statement or wondering whatever happened to your school friends in an old photo. Just sort them into their big, fat categories and get on with the job.

Once you've finished sorting, you need to get rid of paper you no longer need. Do this by setting limits for what you keep.

Set your limits

For your paper to flow in, through and out of your home and office you need to set some limits on how much paperwork you are going to keep in your primary and secondary space. By primary space we mean areas that are close at hand and easy to get to. Shelves above desks, shelves in bookcases, desk surfaces, filing cabinets and cupboards and even areas in kitchens all have potential to be primary storage space for your paper.

Secondary space includes areas up high and down low, backs of cupboards or deep shelves, awkward to get to places, attics, basements, garages, and off site storage. Reference paperwork needs to live in primary space, while archive paperwork can happily live in secondary space.

The big question you need to answer now is: what is your limit? What magic formula will determine how much of each item you keep in primary and secondary storage? The answer to this question, regardless of what it is, will change your life forever.

Now that you can easily see how much is in each sorted category, you are in an ideal position to decide on how much you want to keep. You're in the driver's seat and in control. The best news is that there are only three real ways you can limit your reference items to create a collection that is just right for you. You can mix and match them any way you like as long as you set a limit!

Pick a date

You can limit by date. Simply choose a cut-off date for the item in question. For instance, you might decide to keep the latest 18 months of your bank statements in reference files and to keep the previous five years in archive files. By choosing a date you have a clear demarcation point. This makes it easy to let go of the items that fall outside of your date limit.

Pick a number

You can limit by number. Ask yourself: How many is enough? You may decide that the latest four gas bills, the latest twelve bank statements and the latest three insurance renewals are right for your reference files. You also need to choose the number you will hold in your archive files.

Pick a container

You can limit by the amount of space you want your item or category to occupy. Remember, everything in your home and office is competing for space. Simply decide how much space you want to dedicate to any item or category. For instance, you may decide to fill a display book with recipes you want to try one day. Once the book is full, you have reached your limit.

Can you see how powerful limiting is? Regardless of what limits you set, the flow out is inevitable. Set your limit, reach your limit and then, in order to add items to your file, you must let some paper go. The natural flow of your paper has returned with each simple limit decision.

When choosing your limits take into account your local tax and legal requirements for record keeping. We have included some general guidelines for what to keep and these are in Appendix 3. This may vary from state to state and country to country. You should always seek advice when in doubt about these requirements. Always ensure your limits meet your legal duties.

> **!** What limits will you apply for each of the items you have in your big fat categories? Note your limits against each item on your list of categories.

Once you set a limit you also need to set a rule for what to do when you want to add an item after the limit has been reached. For items you don't need to archive, which is the majority of reference paperwork, apply the 'one-in, one-out' rule. When a new one comes in the oldest one goes out. For items you need to archive you may cull every six or 12 months and move them into archives.

Letting limits lead

Melanie set limits on the number of reference items she keeps. She decided to keep one magazine box full of her subscription garden magazines, so once the box is full, when a new magazine comes in she simply puts the oldest one she has in her paper recycling bin. She set a limit of 18 months for her quarterly gas bills. She loads her file up with the latest 18 months worth of gas bills and when the next one comes in she adds it to the front of her file and throws the oldest one out, leaving her back at her limit. She decided to do an annual cull of bank statements and simply removed the last financial year and archived them. As she adds a year to her archives, she removes the oldest year in her archive collection and shreds the information. Everything is flowing at Melanie's house and she is in charge, making decisions and managing her paper flow every day.

Choosing your reference file containers

Reference files can be placed in a variety of different file containers. Be governed by what you already have, your space, your taste, your budget and the shape and size of the documents you want to file. Feel free to mix and match as much as you like. You can combine categories to form a bigger file. For example by combining the two categories of banking and insurance you create the Banking and Insurance file.

Here are some file container options:

Filing cabinets

Filing cabinets have long been used in homes and offices, they are lockable and house a lot of information. However, if managed poorly, they have a tendency to become cemeteries for paper. If you choose to use a filing cabinet, consider these guidelines and tips:

- Insert one manila folder into every suspension file (sometimes called a hanging file)
- Never overfill the manila folders. Use more suspension files and manila folders as your reference files grow
- Every suspension file requires a label on its tab and an identical label on the manila folder within it
- Only remove the manila folder when using a file, never remove the suspension file
- Use one colour of suspension files for all your reference file categories. Make it a different colour to your recurring action and project files to make for easy identification
- The tabs within each category will sit directly behind each other. Each category should then be staggered across so you can easily see where each category begins and where it ends
- Use a label maker or hand print in dark ink to clearly name files on both the tabs and on the manila folders. For ease of reading use Title Case
- Place items into their manila folder in reverse chronological order with the most recent at the front and the oldest at the back. Place the

manila folder into its suspension file. When adding new items, always add to the front of the file

- You can place files within a category in alphabetical order or by order of importance to you

- When filing items with people's names use an alphabetical system by surname eg Smith, Mary. This type of filing is great for clients and suppliers

- Once set up, create an index of the contents of your filing cabinet by category and items within that category. Keep this in the first suspension file at the front of your filing cabinet's top drawer. Name it 'Filing Index'. Place a copy of this sheet in your ready reference file

- Your filing cabinet may look something like this:

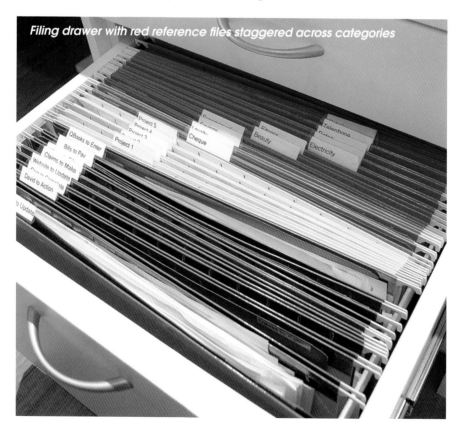

Filing drawer with red reference files staggered across categories

Lever arch folders

These are ideal for most paperwork. They keep things in chronological order, can be read like a book without pages slipping out and are portable. If you choose to use lever arch folders, consider these guidelines and tips:

- lever arch folders require a set of tabbed dividers unless the folder only contains items of one type. For example bank statements for one account only

- sets of tabbed dividers typically come with 5, 8, 10, 12, 20, or 31 tabs. Choose the number of tabs you need, as well as a few more tabs than you need right now to allow for more items later. For example you might open a new bank account and need another tab for new statements

- when placing items into lever arch files allocate the last few tabs for your bulkier or fatter files while the first few tabs are best for thinner files. This saves lifting and turning the fat files to get to the thin files

- assign the first tab in some folders for contact information within the folder. You can place business card sheets behind this tab to collect business cards relating to the entire folder or you may place a list of contacts or important information behind this tab. You will find this very useful for medical and health practitioners' business cards

- leave the last tab as an appendix to the entire folder. You can place items in plastic pockets behind this tab or it can be used for bulkier items. Place things like lease agreements, insurance booklets and any other items that are too bulky for the main section of your folder

- label your tabs using a label maker if possible. You may need to abbreviate and use a smaller size font to fit the tab. If labeling by hand print neatly in dark ink

- create a front sheet, or index, for your tabbed dividers so you can see at a glance what's behind each tab

- enter useful information relating to each tab on the front sheet. For example, the electricity file in your Utilities folder may have the name of your provider, your account number, contact phone number and due dates for accounts; your mobile phone account may have the name of your provider, your account number, your password and your plan expiry date

- the front sheet should give you a snapshot view of the files in your folder which you can update and reprint as you go. Put copies of these sheets in your ready reference file so all file information is in one central place. See our Health file example on page 83 and other examples in appendix 4

- place items behind their tabs in reverse chronological order with the most recent at the front and the oldest at the back

- once you've completed your lever arch folders, consider numbering them. By doing this you will always replace folders on their shelf in exactly the same place after use and you will immediately know when a file goes missing

- when hole punching your pages use a hole punch with a guide set to the relevant page size. Your pages and holes will always line up and will look neat and tidy

- a numbered lever arch folder reference set would look something like this:

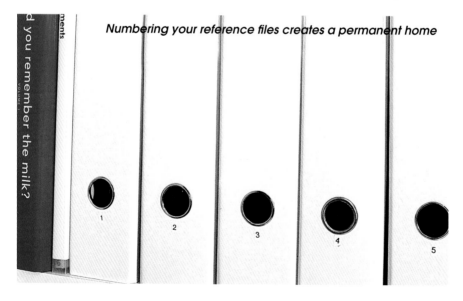

Numbering your reference files creates a permanent home

Magazine boxes

Magazine boxes are ideal for bulky items such as warranties and manuals, magazines, display books and items in rigid plastic pockets. They are portable, keep items vertical and occupy little surface space. If you choose to use magazine boxes for some of your files, consider these guidelines and tips:

- store all loose paper and sets of information in labelled rigid plastic pockets or display books. Loose paper will curl if left standing in magazine boxes for lengthy periods. Paper in magazine boxes needs to be supported

- face the spine of stored items outwards so you can see their titles when removing and replacing files or magazines

- clearly label each magazine box on both front and back so you know what the box contains regardless of the direction it is facing

- magazines boxes are very stable and can also be used as bookends. Just place a couple of filled magazine boxes on a shelf and place a few lever arch folders or books between them

- your magazine boxes may look something like this:

Magazine boxes can also act as bookends

Display books

These are simply books of plastic pockets for inserting items you want to keep. They are good for ready-reference information, important documents, recipes, takeaway menus and special interests. They keep your paperwork clean and tidy. If you choose to use display books for some of your files, consider these guidelines and tips:

- use display books for non-bulky items only
- don't insert more than ten pages into each individual pocket. More than this will put stress on the pockets and they may fall apart
- if you want to store items that are smaller than the pocket itself, simply insert a sheet of blank paper or light card into the pocket to stabilise it first, then add your smaller items
- leave the front pocket empty for a front sheet, title page or table of contents
- label display books on the top of their spines for easy identification. Be consistent in your location and style of labeling to ensure uniformity
- your plastic display book may look something like this:

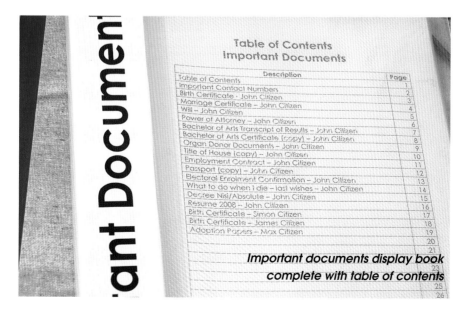

Table of Contents
Important Documents

Description	Page
Table of Contents	1
Important Contact Numbers	
Birth Certificate - John Citizen	2
Marriage Certificate – John Citizen	3
Will – John Citizen	4
Power of Attorney – John Citizen	5
Bachelor of Arts Transcript of Results – John Citizen	6
Bachelor of Arts Certificate (copy) – John Citizen	7
Organ Donor Documents – John Citizen	8
Title of House (copy) – John Citizen	9
Employment Contract – John Citizen	10
Passport (copy) – John Citizen	11
Electoral Enrolment Confirmation – John Citizen	12
What to do when I die – last wishes – John Citizen	13
Decree Nisi/Absolute – John Citizen	14
Resume 2008 – John Citizen	15
Birth Certificate – Simon Citizen	16
Birth Certificate – James Citizen	17
Adoption Papers – Max Citizen	18
	19
	20
	21

Important documents display book complete with table of contents

Storage boxes of varying shapes and sizes

Storage boxes and containers are useful for reference items that are small or of irregular shape and size. Storage boxes are useful for little books, passports, bank deposit books, cheque books, membership booklets, CDs, DVDs, small receipts, photos, business cards and office tools.

If you choose to use storage boxes, consider these guidelines and tips:

- store contents vertically within the box where possible to allow for easy retrieval
- aim to only fill any storage box to about 90 percent of its capacity. You need space to be able to move things in and out of their boxes
- if the box is only partly filled, insert a filler to keep items vertical and stable. For instance if you only have a few CDs in a CD box, you might fill it with some scrunched up paper to ensure the CDs you do have stand up nice and straight until more CDs move in to stabilise the box
- use divider cards to separate items within a box where necessary. For example business cards, DVDs and CDs
- consider having a row of boxes in a bookcase without lids to ensure easy access to contents. Sometimes boxes work best without lids
- label boxes and divider card tabs with a label maker or hand print in dark ink

> **Which combination of file storage will work best for you, based on your needs and available space?**

Storage boxes can be used for tools, small receipts and stationery

Setting up your reference files

Now we will show you how to set up your reference files using some of the most common files in a reference system.

Ready-reference information

A ready-reference file holds all the information you need at your fingertips and is accessed all the time. Think of it as the file that holds all your 'I need it right now' information. It typically contains lists, timetables, important numbers, emergency contact details, babysitter information, checklists and instructions. It should also contain a copy of your master filing lists.

Ready reference at your fingertips in Perspex holder

Sarah's ready reference saves the day

Sarah was on an interstate business trip when her handbag was stolen. She was stranded without money, mobile phone, hotel key, credit cards, camera, driver's licence, notebook, cheque book and make-up. Her worst nightmare had become reality. She managed a call home to her husband and gave him the following instructions: 'Please go to my ready reference file and refer to my 'What's in my Handbag' list and cancel my credit cards'. A few minutes later all her credit cards were cancelled and although Sarah was still very inconvenienced she was much more in control. Having a 'What's in my Handbag' list saved her having to try to remember all the things she routinely carried with her. Since that time Sarah has taken the extra precaution of having her list available to her anywhere, anytime by emailing it to herself. She can now access the information in the event that there is no one at home during a crisis. Sarah's ready reference file continues to grow and evolve as her needs change and evolve. Perfect!

Important documents

Important documents include birth certificates, passports, wills and contracts. Although the contents may differ, an important documents file is essential to everyone. Once you have gathered and reviewed all your important documents you just have to decide what type of storage to use.

A display book is ideal for important documents as they live in their own individual pockets for protection and they are easily picked up to go with you when you need them. Create a 'master list' for the front pocket and then place all your documents into the sleeves one at a time. Create a label for the spine of your display book and your most important file is complete! If they don't all fit into one display book, you could have a series of them sitting in a magazine box.

Here is a list of the types of documents that you could house in your important document file:

- birth certificates
- adoption papers
- christening, baptism, naming certificates
- first communion certificates
- confirmation certificates
- bar mitzvah records
- marriage certificates
- change of name records
- separation and/or divorce records
- custody and maintenance records
- death certificates
- passport details
- visas and work permits
- residency papers
- citizenship papers
- immigration records
- military service records

- wills
- powers of attorney
- funeral plans and death wishes
- qualifications
- titles
- contracts
- mortgages
- loans
- organ donor registration
- electoral enrolment details
- family tree or history

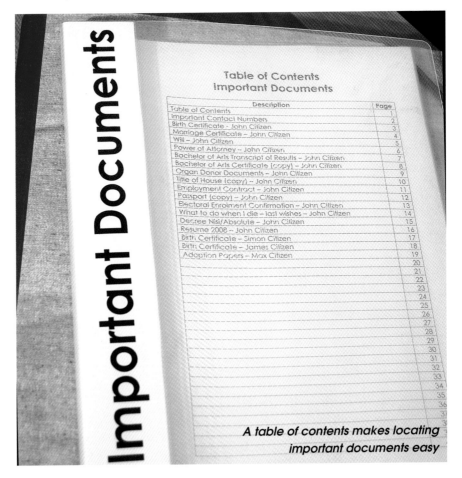

A table of contents makes locating important documents easy

Tips for securing your important information

Keep a duplicate copy of all your important documents at home and another copy elsewhere, just in case. You may feel safer keeping your original house title, will etc. lodged with your solicitor or in a bank safety deposit box. In that case, write a note on the copy document indicating where the original is located, in case you forget, or if someone else needs to access it in your absence.

If you think you will need copies of original records frequently, then make a few copies at one time, certify each one and keep them in your file ready for when you need them.

Banking and finance

This is where you put all your financial information. Let's say you have three bank accounts, one mortgage, one personal loan, two credit cards and one loyalty program. When it comes time to cull your files, after considering your tax and legal requirements, you may decide you want to keep the last six years of bank statements, as well as the mortgage and loan set-up documents, and the last three loyalty statements. So you sort the records into chronological order and place the files in a lever arch folder with labelled tabbed dividers and a front sheet. You decide to keep the last 18 months in your reference file and put the remainder into archives. Your paper is beginning to tell you what it needs and you are able to respond accordingly. Experiment a little to get the right balance between reference and archive.

Utilities or household expenses

Everyone needs a file to keep all their household expenses and everyone will have one that looks a little different from the other. This file is filled with paid bills for household related items like; gas, electricity, water, council rates, insurance, telephone, internet, pay TV and home maintenance. Group them by provider name (e.g. 'Origin Gas') in reverse chronological order. Set a limit for each item in this file, around 18 months is ideal for most non-tax related items. Discard anything outside your limit and place the rest into a lever arch binder with labelled dividers and a front sheet. If you are collecting information to do a household budget, you can use these receipts as well as your bank statements to plan ahead. Your file may have tabs that look like this:

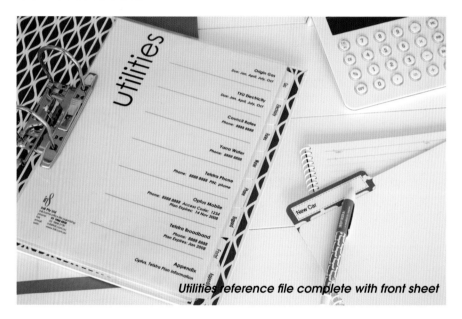

Utilities reference file complete with front sheet

Health

Once you have gathered all your health information together, review the documents one at a time and sort them into logical sub-categories. Cull any unnecessary information. Your finished file may include government and private health funds, medical and health professional contact details, claimed medical receipts from health funds, health history documents for each member of the family, pet information and vet receipts. Lever arch files are ideal for these records. You will need to select a set of tabbed dividers that slightly exceeds the number of sub-categories in this file. You will also need to create a front sheet based on the sub-categories you have created and it may look like this:

health

Medical Contact Details
Business cards for all medical providers, contact sheets

Medicare and Private Health Insurance
Very Healthy Health Fund, Premium Plan
Member No: 1234 9876
Medicare No: 1234 5678 3

Steven's Medical History
Medical Reports, Hospital Stays, Test Results
Steven's X-Rays are in the linen press under the pillows

Clare's Medical History
Medical Reports, Hospital Stays, Test Results
Clare's X-Rays are in the linen press under the sheets

Max's Medical History
Medical Reports, Hospital Stays, Test Results
Max's Health Centre Book is in the top drawer in the study

Dentist – Margaret Fields
Phone: 1234 5678
Orthodontic Plan, Accounts, General tips on teeth
Payment plan expires 30 June

Vet – Doug Miles
Ph: 9876 5432
Receipts

Fido the Dog
Pet Registration, Vaccination Records, Health Records

Health Receipts – after claims have been made
Health Fund Receipts & any non-claimable item receipts
Review at tax time to calculate health rebate

Appendix
Health Insurance Booklet

www.paperflow.com.au

Appendix 4 shows front sheet examples for your most common reference files.

Warren gives his research files a workout

Warren is a fitness fanatic and collects lots of information relating to fitness, nutrition and exercise. He finds it really easy to tear out articles and gather information but he can never find these articles when he wants to share them with fellow fitness fanatics and clients. It's time to get sorted. He pulls all of his fitness information into a couple of magazine boxes and proceeds to sort it into sub-categories. When he takes a good look at his collection he finds he had lots of duplicates and similar articles in each of his sub-categories. Once he sees the whole collection in one place, it's easy to decide what should stay and what should go. He easily culls at least half of it. A lot of information he has kept just for the contact details and web addresses so he places this into his Contacts to Update recurring action file and his Websites to Visit file. He enters the contact information into a new group called 'Fitness Contacts' on his database. He is really impressed with the way all his information is finding its natural place in his system. He uses three display books, one for fitness, one for nutrition and one for exercise and places them into a magazine box. He leaves the first pocket of each display book empty for an index and slips each of his articles into the pockets behind the index page. Then he labels the spines and takes a moment to stand back. He feels really great looking at his finished reference pack. His wife Andrea follows suit with her diet, nutrition, exercise and beauty collection. Their two reference sets now stand side-by-side on the shelf looking as streamlined as their owners!

Children's information

Your magazine box holding your children's information is likely to be crammed with a mixture of documents and memorabilia. The first thing to do is to separate these. Cull each based on your limits. While children are young most people simply incorporate all children's items in with their own. For example, children's bank statements would be housed with all other family bank accounts, their shares would be in the family share file, their birth certificate would be in the family important document file. Paper storage requirements change as children get older. They may be driving, working, have a car, phone accounts and many of the other adult trappings, but they may still be living at home. Once a child reaches their final years at school, it's good to start separating their files from the family files. You can create files containing specific information relating to each child so that they have everything sorted by the time they leave the family nest.

Anne and Steve get straight 'A's' for school files

Anne and Steve work full-time and have three children. Two of their children are at school and one at pre-school so they want to set up a school filing system to use over the next 18 years, applying some smart rules to keep the paper under control.

Rather than trying to cram everything into one ring binder, they separate their information into three sets of files. Looking at their school document needs, they decide on a magazine box with several display books inside.

The first display book holds everyday information regarding logistics of school life. As both children are at the same school, they only need one display book for current class lists, tuckshop menus and price lists, uniform requirements and sizes, permission slips, class and extra-curricular timetables, parent contact details, car pooling information, a school handbook, emergency numbers, school receipts and a schedule of fees.

Each plastic sleeve in the display book is labelled with the contents (e.g. 'Class List') so that if a piece of paper is removed, they know what's missing. The display book lives in a magazine box labelled 'School' in their study. Each year, they update it with new information, but the basic type of information stays the same.

They use the second display book for each child's academic progress, reports and achievements, filed in chronological order.

They file each term report in separate, labelled pockets, taking care not to overfill the pockets so the book was manageable. Each child has one book for primary school, which they can archive when they reach secondary school.

Once Anne and Steve's children have graduated from school they will have a complete set of school reports to refer to. They will have copies of all class lists and they can either add any additional study at university and courses undertaken or start a new file.

While the first two display books contain current or historical information, the third display book is used for planning. In this file they keep goals for their children, information about programs and activities of interest, future academic information, extra reading lists and websites to support learning. This keeps them a few steps ahead and serves as an excellent tool for their child's development.

Tax

When it comes to tax, people fall into two main groups: one group thinks of tax as a project undertaken once a year; the other group collects tax-relevant information all year.

Those in the first group file their information into their regular reference files. They place bank statements in Banking and Finance and health insurance information in Health. Once a year they move through these files and extract the information required to lodge their tax returns. It's a good idea to keep a tax checklist in your ready reference file so you don't forget an item. You could even have these items colour coded or highlighted within the file as a visual reminder; a red dot against an item would mean to include it for tax.

People in the other group like filing all their tax documentation together throughout the year. They have a reference file called 'Tax' with some sub-divided categories, and all tax information goes in there.

> **!** Which group do you belong to? Both methods work well, but you need to choose which you prefer and then set up your files accordingly.

Warranties and manuals

Like many people, you probably have a big collection of warranties and instruction manuals that you have collected over the years, a large portion of which may be obsolete. Set yourself up with a pack of expanding pockets (refer to the gallery of tools on page 159), a label maker and a couple of magazine boxes and wade through your past purchases. This is a good job to do while watching television. Look at each briefly, decide what to keep and what to toss in the recycle bin, and place the keepers into their own labelled pocket and then into a magazine box. You might end up with one magazine box for all electrical items and one for all computer-related items. From now on, make it your practice to throw out old warranties or manuals at the same time as you get rid of your old or unused belongings.

Tips for keeping track of receipts and warranties

For purchases with a warranty period, staple the receipt to the back of the warranty so they are together. This saves a lot of shuffling around if the fridge stops working two years down the track. When purchasing a number of big-ticket items at one time, ask the shop assistant to print one receipt per item. Now you can easily staple each receipt to the appropriate warranty, instead of having one receipt with six items listed on it.

Never lose your instructions again!

Set Top Box

Digital Camera

Plasma TV

Small receipts

Go to your handbag or wallet right now and pull out all your small receipts. Throw away all those receipts that you will never need again. The rest might need to be kept for a certain period for an exchange or return, or as evidence of items purchased for tax or insurance purposes. So what should we do with the ones we want to keep?

Our minimum level of organising small receipts is to simply assign a shoebox-sized box with 12 envelopes inside. Each day when you get home, empty your small receipts into this box. At the end of each month, take your small receipts out of the box and place them into one of your empty envelopes. Write the month and the year on the envelope and place it back inside the box. Repeat this process for 12 months and then bundle the envelopes up with a rubber band. Now, if the jacket you bought starts to come apart at the seams, you simply go to the envelope for the month that you purchased the jacket and retrieve the receipt so you can return it to the store. Easy!

Just like everything in your system, set limits for receipts and once your limit is reached, throw your receipts away. For example, you may like to have the last two years receipts ready at hand. Once that limit is reached, play the one in one out game with your envelopes.

Tips for small receipts

- Highlight or circle the date and the item purchased on the receipt so you can see it at a glance.

- Small receipts can fade easily, especially in plastic pockets. Photocopy or scan significant small receipts, for art and jewellery for example, to prevent losing important information over time.

- Instead of going through all your old receipts as you clear up your piles, why not: gather them all up, bundle them into a large envelope and write 'All small receipts up until (enter date)'. Now put that envelope in your archives (see Chapter 6) or go back to it once your filing system is humming along. The envelope and their contents can be whittled away while you watch television. The key is not to sweat the small stuff – don't over-organise items you will rarely use or need. The majority of small receipts are unnecessary within three months of purchasing most everyday items. Let them die a natural death.

Contacts

Everyone needs an address book or a computer-based list of contact details for family, friends and business associates. Business cards can either be kept in a business card holder or the details transferred into your address book or computer. Mostly people categorise their contacts in alphabetical order. You can also put contacts into meaningful categories. For example, 'interior design contacts' might get listed under 'I'. From now on you will be placing all new contact information into your Contacts to Enter recurring action file. However, you may also have a backlog of contacts needing to be entered into your computer or you may want to update your old address book to a new one. You're staring at a pile and wondering if you'll ever have time to get to it? Did you know that the easiest way to get the job done is by breaking it down? When adding contact details to your computer or address book, simply set a daily target that you'll enter until they're all done. For example, you may decide to enter eight entries per day. Similarly, when transferring from one address book to another set yourself a target of completing one letter of the alphabet each day. Breaking the job down into bite sized chunks makes the job so much easier and adds an element of fun as well.

℮ Online vs Offline – keeping it simple

Managing your reference information will be so much easier if you use the same filing approach on your computer as in your paper based system. Now that you have set up your paper based reference files, with a few clicks of the mouse, you can re-arrange your 'soft copy' reference information in the same way. Simply create a folder called Reference Files on your computer. In this folder, create a series of new reference folders using the same file names as your paper files. If your computer files are in a big mess, then simply create some big fat categories which will make it much easier to sort through. For example: Finances, Work, Home Improvements, Children, etc. You can create a file called 'The Pile as at (a certain date)' and drag and drop all your files into that one big folder. Simply set yourself a daily limit to work through it file by file, finding a new home for each document as you go, or deleting old stuff. Storage space is usually no problem with computer files, but they can quickly become difficult to work with if you keep too much stuff. To avoid this problem, do the same as you have done with your paper files, set up limits for how long you keep your 'soft copy' files and regularly cull. All the principles we have outlined in this chapter are the same whether you are organising the piles on your computer or in your office.

Cruise control

Let's look at your results for this chapter. You have:

- [ ] decided what reference files are right for you
- [ ] created a list of your reference files on paper
- [ ] sorted your reference paper into big fat categories
- [ ] set limits for all items in each category
- [ ] decided on the most appropriate storage for the items you are keeping
- [ ] created a master list of your reference files
- [ ] set up appropriate reference files on your computer

Your reference files are now set up, have defined limits and items are flowing smoothly in, through and out of your home or office.

Further downstream

Most of the reference files we have tackled here will sit in your 'primary space' to access on a daily basis if needed. In the next chapter we're going to tackle the paper that you like to hang on to, but don't need to access regularly. This next chapter will help you deal with your legal obligations as well as those sentimental reasons that compel us to keep certain paper in our lives. You will now create your archive files and manage the flow of paper leaving your home and office. Read on, follow our instructions and stay in control of your paper files forever.

> Simplicity is making the journey of this life with just baggage enough.
>
> *Charles Dudley Warner*

Onwards and outwards

I don't need this certificate right now but I would like to keep it for when the children grow up. What should I do with my old travel diary from the trip we took 5 years ago? Do I need to shred unwanted paper? We still have all our documents from every house we lived in, should we keep them? I always seem to leave the house without the letters I need to post. Where should I keep old press clippings from when I was president of my professional association? I have no idea where all my old school photos are and I would love to have them for the reunion I am attending next week. Having my divorce papers in my office is depressing me, what should I do with all those documents? How do I store or dispose of paper that has passed its usefulness?

Everyone has questions like these. When left unresolved, these questions can lead us to either hang on unnecessarily to our paper or conversely, throw out items that are precious or sentimental, just because we don't know where to put them. We are now going to help you decide what you want to do with the paper flowing out of your action stations and reference files.

Your three choices

Once paper has served its purpose in each of its action stations and reference files, it needs to continue on its journey towards its ultimate destination, out of your life completely.

To keep your paper moving, you can choose one of three paths to send it on its journey. You can:

1. Keep it
2. Pass it on
   or
3. Bin it!

Whichever direction your paper takes, there are some tips, tricks and guidelines that will help you move it smoothly and send it quickly on its way.

Keep it – archives

An archive is simply an infrequently used or old reference file or keepsake. Archives are items you want or need, but not right now or in the immediate future. The beauty of separating your archives from the rest of your system is that you free up valuable primary storage space and you put your less-valuable secondary storage space to good use. You won't mind walking a few extra steps to get to your archives if you only need to access them a couple of times a year.

Follow these seven simple steps and create an archiving system that really meets your needs and is easy to access:

Step One – Decide what you're going to archive

Any kind of paper can be archived. Some paper is kept as a legal requirement, while other paper is kept as a matter of choice. Here are some examples of typical archive files:

- *Old financial records* – bank, loan and credit card statements, cheque stubs, superannuation statements, investment records, tax records (income, expenses, returns), and some insurance policies
- *Property records* – purchase and sale documents, plans and drawings, investment property records, capital improvement information and major renovation documents
- *Legal records* – litigation records, court orders, contracts, divorce papers and child support information
- *Employment records* – old position descriptions, contracts, military service records, letters of employment and termination
- *Records of old purchases* – houses you have lived in, cars you have owned, collections you have had
- *Diaries* – old diaries, address books, note books, journals
- *Travel* – holiday or travel keepsakes, brochures, maps, travel diaries, old passports, tickets and itineraries
- *Keepsakes* – cards, invitations, letters, booklets from weddings, funerals, christenings and graduations, old photographs, autographs, press clippings, tickets and theatre programs
- *Family history* – old family records, letters, press clippings, events and diaries
- *Children* – school records, art, class lists, awards and achievements, birthday cards, special clothing

Of course you do not have to archive all of this! Remember our golden rule from chapter one – 80 per cent of what you keep, you never refer to again.

For most people, archives consist of a box or two containing past tax information and banking records as well as some extra storage for memorabilia.

> **What are you going to archive? Make a list of those items in your notebook.**

When should I archive?

You know it's archive time when your reference files are filled to overflowing but the items contained in them are still required for financial, legal or sentimental reasons. If you keep celebration cards or holiday memorabilia, archive time is several weeks after those events. An annual review of all your reference files will reveal which items need to be archived. Bank statements, tax information, and other 'need to keep' files can be processed annually following the lodgement of tax returns.

Anita breathes life into her mum's old keepsakes

Anita's mother was going through some old photos, letters and memorabilia she brought from Germany when she emigrated. She was about to throw them out but as soon as Anita saw them her eyes lit up and they talked about the war years and life for her parents arriving in Australia in 1948. Those records would be Anita's only link to Germany once her mother died, so they decided to keep them. Anita's mother translated the letters and other documents and wrote a story for future generations to read. Anita scanned the old photos and collated them with her mother's story to include in a coffee table book for the family, using free software she found on the internet. Anita felt so relieved and excited that such an important part of the family's history would be beautifully preserved.

Tips for preserving family memories

Perhaps an event in your life is so precious that you want to turn it into a book. This has now become an easy and effortless option with free software available online. You simply pull together the 'raw materials' you have stored in various locations around your house, for example, photos, letters, tickets, invitations and other memorabilia and write the story or captions for each. You then follow the steps online to insert the items into a template of your choice to create a coffee table book that gets shipped to you. The benefit of a book like this is that everyone can share your memories without the original items getting worn or damaged. You can also give copies to those people who shared the event with you.

Other options for preserving a special memory are creating a DVD on your computer or even just a dedicated display book with all your items. It's advisable to professionally scan and back up precious documents in case the original is damaged.

When keeping family information, carefully assess what you want to leave as a legacy to others and what you want to keep for yourself. Always ask others what they would like to have left for them. Ask other family members what they collect and have in their archives. You may like to consolidate your collections or appoint one family member as keeper of certain information, particularly genealogy.

Step Two – Create your rules – how much and how long?

Gather everything in one place. Take a good look through what you have. Remember not to dawdle down memory lane – stay focused. Use magazine boxes or containers to sort what you have into broad categories, for example, 'photos', 'wedding' and 'school memorabilia'. Keep items as vertical as possible to minimize the amount of surface space required for both sorting and storing.

Set some goals and limits around what you do and don't want to keep. The same three methods to limiting your reference files also apply to your archives: you can limit by date, by number or by space.

For example, you may choose to keep the past five years of tax and banking. By assigning this cut-off date it is easy to limit the amount in archives. You may decide to keep the best 10 pieces of artwork for each child, a set of four birthday cards for each birthday or any other pre-set number of items to keep in your archives.

By setting a limit, your archives don't get out of control. You may have a shelf in your garage allocated to archives which means you are limited to the amount of space on that shelf. You may have three boxes in which to store your archives so you are limited to the amount of space within those containers. So for each category of archive simply set an appropriate limit for what you want to keep. You can mix and match limits to suit your needs and preferences.

There are rules on how long you must keep certain documents for tax or legal reasons. As the rules differ across many countries, we have not covered all the detail here, but a rule of thumb can be found in appendix 3 on page 153. To be absolutely certain, consult your accountant or lawyer.

> **!** **For each of your archive categories, how much are you going to keep and for how long?**

Tips for a memory box to treasure

It's a great idea to have a memory box for each family member to keep cards, letters, mementos, old passports, school records and other sentimental items for reflection and sharing. Once the memory box is full, you can either start another one if you have the space, or create some limits, for example one box per family member. Then simply apply some rules from Step Two 'one in, one out' to limit the amount kept.

Sonia and Steve's brilliant brag books

Sonia and Steve have three children and are very proud and involved in each of their children's activities. Over the years they have collected a plethora of sports ribbons and trophies, artwork, reports, clippings, birthday cards and letters. The twins were still at primary school and their oldest child had started university. It was time to sort through the mountain of school memorabilia found around the house. First, they grouped together each child's items so they could clearly see how much 'stuff' each child had. They then created smaller groups of similar information and archived it. School reports and educational awards and certificates went into acid free display books and then into magazine boxes. They grouped celebration cards and put them into a storage box without too much sorting as only the favourites had been kept. There was room in this box for other paper keepsakes like important event tickets, programs for performances and developmental records. Whenever the children want to look back at some precious memories, they will find them beautifully and lovingly preserved.

Step Three – Choose your containers

Have you ever been horrified to discover that your treasured old letters and documents have faded, discoloured or become brittle? When choosing containers for long term paper storage, you need to look for 'archival quality' containers. As paper is made mainly from wood, rag or recycled paper or a combination of those, it can disintegrate over time. Follow these guidelines and tips for the best storage solution.

Choosing the right containers depends on how long you want to keep the contents. Items which only need to be stored for less than ten years or so, such as tax information, most likely don't require archival quality storage. The following options will do: suspension files, manila folders, display books, lever arch folders, envelopes, document boxes, archive boxes and plastic containers.

For anything you want to keep for a long time (i.e. ten or more years), or even for future generations, you'll need to take more care. First, work out the type of container you will need by looking at the size and shape of the items. You can store large documents such as maps or artwork, either flat or rolled up. You could fit information such as all the houses you lived in or all of your family history into a series of display books, folders, or boxes. It's a good idea to store similar types of material together.

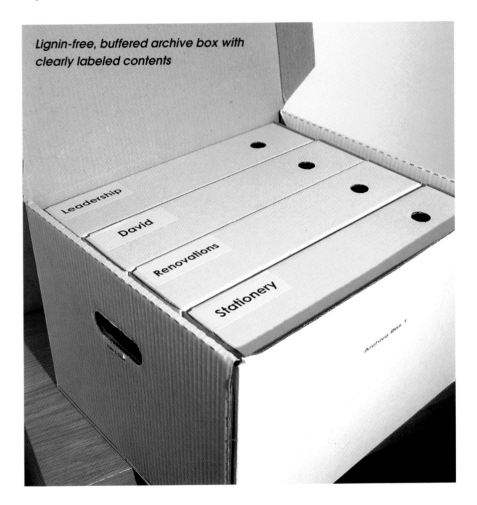

Lignin-free, buffered archive box with clearly labeled contents

Tips for storing oversized items

Some of the items you want to store might be oversized, for example, prints, maps, broadsheet newspapers, and other large items. Since most people don't own a set of map drawers, consider rolled storage. Simply roll your items around tubes, ensuring the tube is longer than the rolled object and once rolled up firmly, wrap with neutrally coloured or buffered paper to protect it from abrasion. You can then put these inside a larger acid-free tube for added protection. Store tubes horizontally or vertically and label them with a list of contents.

When choosing a container for each of your categories, make sure it's made of the right material. Many office stationery items, which appear 'protective', actually damage paper. Your choice comes down to cardboard or plastic. The following few paragraphs are technical, but as we're talking about preserving very precious or important documents, you want to make the right choice. So bear with us!

Cardboard

When using cardboard boxes, beware of the acid factor. Cardboard boxes and cardboard generally become acidic over time, potentially damaging your paper. What you're looking for is lignin-free, buffered cardboard boxes or folders. Here's what those terms mean. 'Buffering' is the adding of agents to the paper or cardboard during production which neutralise the acids that would cause breakdown and discolouration of your paper over time, affecting its archival quality. For those who really want to make sure, buffering will raise the pH level to 8.5 which is the ideal level for long term paper storage. Acid-free paper should have a pH level of 6.5, which is your bare minimum. Lignin is a chemical substance found naturally in wood which bonds the cellulose in wood, making wood (and therefore paper) stronger. However lignin breaks down over time, turning paper brown and releasing harmful acids. So using lignin-free, buffered cardboard boxes or folders is your very best choice when it comes to cardboard.

For standard document storage, the best option is manila folders that are low-lignin and buffered. For optimal shelf life, keep the contents to a maximum of about 15 sheets per folder. Choose a neutral colour. The folders should then be placed in archival-quality document storage boxes as close to the size of the folders as possible. All folders in each box should be the same size. The other alternative is the standard filing cabinet equipped with suspension files.

Tips for Success – storing newspaper clippings ✅

Most newsprint is highly acidic and will deteriorate over time, turning it yellow and brittle. So to keep old family or historic articles, the best approach is to photocopy the article on archival quality paper before filing it away with the original. Store these flat in art folio holders available from art stores.

Plastic

Plastic boxes are also good to use for storing paper, so long as they are free of materials that may damage the paper. The plastics used in general stationery products vary greatly in chemical stability. Those made of polyester, polypropylene, and polyethylene are generally safe to use for storing paper and photos. Plastic sleeves allow both sides of a page to be viewed without touching the original. Ventilation holes in plastic boxes can ventilate and dilute the acidic byproducts of decay.

The choice of paper versus plastic containers may ultimately come down to a compromise between protection against handling and protection against chemical damage.

Other materials to watch out for are lamination, PVC, contact and adhesive. Many self adhesive photo album pages are highly acidic and should never be used for valuable items. Coloured ribbon and folders may stain paper if wet. Staples and metal fasteners could rust and cause tearing. Rubber bands are known to cut into paper and to perish and become sticky over time. The glue on manila envelopes can damage photos. Sticky notes could leave a sticky residue which attracts dirt, mould and insect eggs.

Take care to keep photo-sensitive paper, such as small receipts and faxes away from plastic and light. If this information is critical, photocopy the item so it's legible for longer.

If you store items in closed plastic containers, make sure there are ventilation holes to reduce any dampness or mould build up. Place crystal anti-humectant sachets in containers to absorb moisture and preserve the contents. These sachets are available at most supermarkets.

When filling your containers, fill them to 80-90 per cent capacity. If you over-stuff them you may damage documents when pulling them out or replacing them. If you under-fill the boxes the paper can roll, flop and curl and become damaged. Fill the remaining space of partially full boxes with spacer boards from conservation suppliers or you can use everyday objects, such as books, to fill the box.

Be kind to yourself and think ahead to how you're going to access the container. Once filled, a container should not be too heavy if it is to be stored on a top shelf. We recommend a greater quantity of smaller boxes rather than a smaller quantity of larger boxes if weight is an issue. Large boxes are great for lighter things like children's stuffed toys but terrible for heavy books, unless they are stored down low.

> **What types of containers will you use? Do you need different sizes and shapes?**

Step Four – Label your containers

Label each container on all sides to ensure visibility regardless of how the item is placed in its location. You can use a general title, a detailed content list, a number or any combination of these. For example a box of school work could be labelled 'School Assignments' or it could be labeled with a list of all the school assignments in the box, or just have a number and be called 'Box 10'. What title you use will depend on the sensitivity and privacy you feel about the contents of your archives.

For every archive in your system you need to create a list of contents in your ready reference file to cross reference with the titles of each archive. It's also good to have a copy of the list inside each archive, the lid is a good place for this.

Labelling can be done using a label maker or permanent marker. The key is that the labels are large enough to see and identify from standing position and that they are suitable for the environment in which they are stored. For example, waterproof labels may be required for damp areas and to prevent labels falling off, while a marker pen may be best for hot and dry areas.

Step Five – Assign a location

The enemies of document storage are humidity, temperature, UV light, dust and dirt, so let these be the first consideration when determining the best location. The optimal paper storage temperature is 13 to 27 degrees Celsius or 55 to 80 degrees Fahrenheit and humidity should remain at between 40 to 60 per cent.

The next consideration is your available space and the number of archives needing storage. Can they fit in a cupboard? Should they go in the garage? Can they go to a family member for safekeeping if space is limited or inappropriate?

Use the backs of deep cupboards, high spaces, low spaces and even awkward corners for your archive files and other infrequently used items. They're the 'inside' options. Garages, off-site storage facilities or extended family's houses are some 'outside' options. To help you decide, think about how frequently you'll want to access the contents. You might want to keep school reports closer at hand than the children's artwork, for example, which you can store away until the children are grown up.

Step Six – Write a master list

So you don't forget what you've archived, it's a good idea to create a master list (see the example below). The key is to keep it simple, regardless of how complex your archive collection may be. When you're accessing your archives, you will know which box to select by scanning the keywords or contents list. Keep your archive master list in your ready-reference file with all your other filing information. You will never have to search for those nostalgic keepsakes ever again.

Box	Description	Keywords or Contents	Location
1	Family history	Genealogy, family tree	Top shelf of bookcase in study
2	School records	Primary, secondary, tertiary, class lists, photos, year books	Cupboard in spare room
3	School uniforms	Hats, blazer, summer dress, tie	Cupboard in spare room
4	Tax returns	2009, 2008, 2007, 2006, 2005	Top shelf in garage

Keeping track of contents

Elizabeth is custodian of a few generations of past family history. She has created an extensive archive system for her family history and major family events. Her personal archives include purchase and sale documents, renovation details and photographs for each property she has owned; records of the 1956 and 2000 Olympic Games she attended; and school records and school uniform items for reunions and reminiscing. To keep on top of it all she has a master list of everything in her archive boxes. Instead of labelling them with descriptions of their contents, she has numbered her boxes and updates the master list every time she adds or removes something. If family members want to retrieve anything it's always an easy process, thanks to her handy contents tracker.

Step Seven – Make an appointment to cull!

Don't forget to regularly cull your archives. It's best to ask your accountant or legal advisor how long to keep documents such as old tax records. Review your list of contents annually to see if some of the items in your archives have passed their use by date and are no longer required. You will know exactly where to go to remove any unwanted excess and you can simply update your master list as you go.

Scanning copies of documents is a good way of holding on to information without taking up space. Keep the electronic archives on your computer and back them up frequently. Set up a folder called 'Archives' in your electronic reference folder.

> **What date are you going to review your archive list and cull anything past its use by date?**

Tips for handling old documents

Take extra care when handling old documents. Use gloves, and consider visiting an archivist for specialist information on how best to preserve old records. Scan fading documents so you preserve the contents before they fade away completely. Whatever you have today is in the best condition it will ever be, so preserve what you can.

Martha's memorable move

Martha is moving into a retirement home and has limited space for her collection of family keepsakes. She invites family members over for a family keepsake handover. Each family member is given an opportunity to select a number of items from her collection. She has old newspapers, magazines, her school records and an invitation from a former Prime Minister, as well as an extensive collection of football autographs and memorabilia. She even has a cup commemorating The Beatles tour to Australia. She sends items that her family don't want to a historic society, a museum, a football club and a theatre group, who welcome the items into their collections.

Pass it on

Some paper simply needs to go to the right person at the right time, such as items to be lodged, claimed, returned, submitted, presented, given, paid or posted. How can you store this paper so that it reaches its destination in a timely and effective fashion? The answer is to set up an out-bag or an out-tray! We showed you how to set up the out-bag in Chapter 3 page 41 to ensure your recurring action items get to the right place at the right time. Read on for other ways to ensure your paper makes the journey onwards and outwards.

Out-bag ready to go

The out-tray

An out-tray is simply a tray that holds items leaving the home or office. Simply set up a specific place for your out-tray and remember to take the appropriate items out when going to appointments and other places. You can use a traditional in-tray, a magazine box or any other container to suit your space and decor. The main thing is to have a designated and exclusive place for all things going out!

Boomerang paper

Some items leave your files permanently and other items come back in a slightly different form; for example, your prescriptions either expire or repeats come back into your system; your forms may come back as passports, licences or tickets; your claims may come back as receipts or cheques; your gift vouchers may result in more receipts, instructions or warranties.

What do you do with all the stuff that comes back? It's simple – it all goes back into your in-tray and you process items on your designated days through your action station. Now you can see how paper flows in, through and out, and sometimes back again.

Bin it

Just because paper is filed away neatly in your home or office doesn't mean it has to stay. Paper should only stay for as long as it serves a real need or purpose and not a moment more. Many items can leave as soon as they arrive. Don't let paper hang around unnecessarily, moving it from place to place just because you can't make a decision. Paper leaves our

system from the in-tray, from our recurring action files, from our projects and from our reference files. Simply ask any piece of paper: Do I really need you from this point forward? If the answer is 'no', then let it go!

You have two basic choices here: you can adopt a day-to-day approach or an annual approach to culling paperwork. The day-to-day approach means that every time you open a file to add something, you take something out (one-in, one-out), which is great for things you don't need to keep beyond 18 months or so. An annual approach requires an annual review of all items and the culling of unnecessary paperwork in one session, which is great for tax-related paperwork, in particular. Remember, you may need to shred any personal information before placing it in the recycling bin.

Letting go of paper is easier said than done for some people. Many people attach a lot of emotion to paperwork, particularly items relating to family and friends. You can keep as much or as little as you like, as long as it has a place to live. If you don't have the space or it is causing you grief, refer back to the advice on setting limits in chapter 5, page 67.

Cruise control

It's time to review what you've done while reading this chapter. You have:

- [ ] decided what you're going to archive
- [ ] set limits and created rules for how much to keep and for how long
- [ ] chosen containers suited to the contents you're archiving
- [ ] clearly labelled your archive containers with a label or a number
- [ ] assigned the most suitable location for your archives based on what you're keeping
- [ ] created a master list of all your archive contents and placed this in your ready reference file
- [ ] scheduled time to add, cull and review your archives at least annually
- [ ] made good use of the recycling bin!

Further downstream

You've now travelled through the *Paper Flow* journey and have one last place to go. Your *Paper Flow* system will work in any home or office environment. Now it's time to bring it all together and make it work in your unique situation. In the next chapter we will show you how to turn your *Paper Flow* into *Office Flow*.

7

> He is happiest, be he king or peasant
> who finds peace in his home.
>
> *Goethe*

Put *Paper Flow* to work anywhere

We've shown you how to set up *Paper Flow*, the world's best paper management system, but many of you may now look at your work station and think 'This still doesn't look or feel quite the way I want it.' After working through *Paper Flow*, it is perfectly natural that you will find there are changes you want to make to your workstation. This chapter is going to show you how to put *Paper Flow* to work in any environment, be it an area under the stairs, a set of portable files in a car, a corner of the kitchen bench or an office on the 25th floor.

The best thing about *Paper Flow* is that it will work in every place and for everyone, regardless of where your paperwork is located. No more excuses that you don't have a dedicated office space – you don't need one. All you need is somewhere to work while you are processing your paper and somewhere to put your stuff when it's not being worked on. From now on your paper will flow smoothly, regardless of your situation.

The world of work has changed dramatically. Gone are the days where you only work in one dedicated place. Thanks to technology, you can now work wherever you want and whenever you want.

So, how do the best offices, work spaces and situations function? Take a look in this chapter and put your work space through its paces!

Creating office flow

Have you ever been in an office or space that just seemed to 'click' with you, where you really felt that 'Wow!' factor? That seemingly intangible ingredient that makes an office 'click' is simply *Office Flow. Office Flow* is a combination of physical, functional and emotional elements, which together create an efficient and comfortable environment.

The average person spends the majority of their week working, which is why your work space has such a huge impact on your general wellbeing. If all your physical office needs are met; you've got the right furniture, technology and equipment but you can't reach your action files from your main desk position, then it's going to annoy you every day. Likewise, if you've addressed the physical and functional elements of your office space, but it's lacking your warmth, personality and soul, then you're going to feel uninspired. When the physical, functional and emotional elements are working in harmony, you will have achieved your own version of *Office Flow.*

To help you create *Office Flow,* work through the steps below. Take time to answer some questions, view your work space with a fresh pair of eyes and create an ideal work space for you, without needing to spend lots of time and money.

First, go and look at the work space you currently use to process paperwork and pretend you're seeing it for the first time.

Step 1: Let's get physical!

Take a look now at your office and consider its layout, lighting, temperature, noise, colour and storage. These questions might help you:

1   Are you comfortable in this spot and is there enough light?

2   Are you able to concentrate on tasks and see them through to completion?

3   Is there sufficient room to undertake each of your tasks?

4   Is there enough space to accommodate your paperwork collection?

5   Can you easily access and replace your paperwork?

6   Is your paper storage area in keeping with the look and feel of the room it is in?

If you answered 'no' to any of these questions, it's time to give your office a physical makeover. Let's explore six typical situations to show you how others have conquered some physical office challenges. You can then follow some guidelines to identify and set up the perfect office for you.

Office flow in a cupboard

Rachael lives in a small one-bedroom apartment that was previously full of 'stuff', detracting from the atmosphere she wanted to create. There were paper piles everywhere, and she had limited storage space that she had to use wisely. So she decided to convert the large linen press in her entrance hall and use it for her paper storage. She moved the towels and sheets to the cupboards in her bedroom, and then cleaned out the linen cupboard and adjusted a few shelves. Rachael placed her files on the shelves and used a cutlery tray to house her daily tools. Now, when Rachael needs to do her paperwork, she simply opens the cupboard, retrieves the files she

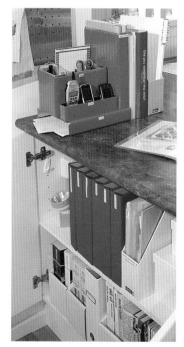

needs and works on her laptop at the dining room table. She has dedicated a shelf in the cupboard for storing her laptop and cables when not in use. The cupboard needed to have a light installed along with power points for her scanner and printer. She also fixed a dedicated power board to the wall for any items requiring charging. Rachael's simple changes have made the world of difference to her *Office Flow*.

Office flow in the kitchen

Close the doors and this office in a cupboard simply disappears

Sarah has three children and works part-time in an office, but needs to catch up on work after hours at home. To get work done without being away from her family, she set up a kitchen office. Her laptop sits in a drawer under the breakfast bar. Above that, a cupboard stores her action files and paperwork, as well as all of her important family information, such as the family calendar and children's school notices. A stool sits under the bench and her phone and in-tray are the only things that sit on the bench top. Sarah is able to undertake many paper tasks and still supervise her children while they play, do homework or watch TV in the family room or kitchen. Her kitchen office takes into account her family situation and current lifestyle needs.

Home office flow

Anne works part-time and has two boys at primary school and a busy home and social life to manage. In her study, all her reference files are lined up in matching binders on a bookshelf on one wall and her desk against another wall. The layout suits the room and provides good lighting and access to power points. She has a laptop with wireless internet, and a 'toolbox' that contains all her tools and writing implements. When her sons are in bed on Thursday nights she goes into her study and completes all her household paperwork. If Anne wants to watch a TV show on Thursday nights, she just grabs her laptop, her files and toolbox and works on a table in the living room. This takes her a bit longer to complete her tasks, but she doesn't mind because she's enjoying herself while getting her tasks done.

The thing Anne loves about her home office is that she can close the door and separate business from pleasure and she can move office items easily

Home offices can be set up in many ways. This office belongs to a couple who run a small business

throughout the home whenever she likes. Her version of *Office Flow* gives her privacy, flexibility and mobility.

Mobile office flow

Richard works in business sales for a large telecommunications company. He spends most days on the road seeing clients and reporting back to the sales force at head office. His job performance is based on the quality of his interactions and meeting deadlines. His workstation moves between the car, coffee shops and clients' offices, while his paperwork location is a portable file box and a briefcase kept in his car. He simply rotates client files into the box on a daily basis. His reference material; standard forms, price lists, brochures and procedures, lives in compartments in his briefcase. His laptop holds additional files that he can access anywhere. Richard has conquered the issues faced by many who have mobile offices: he has the right information and tools at his fingertips wherever he goes. He's on the move, in control and working effectively with a portable file box, briefcase and laptop.

Use a portable file to transport files in your car

Office flow between office and home

An interior designer, Catherine has both a rental office and a home office. She had originally thought that moving into a dedicated rental office would solve all her storage and working problems. However, confusion set in, causing her to forget important items between locations. While the new office allowed her to have all her samples, books, files and desk in one location, it meant she really had to think a lot more about what she needed where and when. She set up her computers so she could access files whether at home or in the office and she purchased a stylish cabin bag with wheels from a luggage store to transport samples, files and catalogues between home, office and clients. Her confusion has been replaced by an office flow solution that suits her work style and image.

Shared office flow

Lee and Margaret run a consultancy business from their home office. Their two children are at university, and they work in the business during semester breaks. Initially sharing the office space and resources was frustrating for all, so they got together and decided on where to put particular items, then named files and added labels and signs. Each person has their own workstation area with an in-tray and a notice board. Margaret is responsible for handling all the paperwork and the household recurring action items, and the other household members know what their responsibilities are and where their important information is. Everyone has a list of the reference files which is updated as necessary. By using a common language, clear labelling, and individual workstations, the family is working as a team.

Your optimal office

Now we've seen how other people have conquered their office shortcomings, here are some guidelines that you can use to identify your issues and solve your office challenges:

- *Layout* – a good layout will make it easy to access information, work on tasks and manoeuvre around the office. It's useful to sketch up a layout of your office or workstation area and play around with the positioning of your furniture and equipment. On that layout, note the position of items like power points, heating ducts, lighting, air vents, windows, doors and built-in furniture.

- *Lighting* – Is your natural, fixed and portable lighting adequate for varying times of day and night and for varying activities? Extra lighting or a change to window fittings could be just the thing you need.

- *Temperature* – Your physical comfort is affected by temperature, and so are many items you store in your office. How hot or cold does the room get over the course of a day and the seasons of the year? Is there anything in your space that could be adversely affected by temperature variation, direct sunlight or temperature extremes such as photos or computer equipment? Consider whether you need additional heating, cooling or insulation.

> **What do you need to do to improve the layout, lighting and temperature in your office?**

- *Noise* – Now sit in your office and notice the sounds around you. Some sounds may stimulate you, some may sooth you and yet others may annoy you. Noise can be reduced by changing locations, double glazing of windows, insulation, sound proofing or by moving the source of the noise. If the source of the noise is your neighbour, a friendly chat can usually fix the problem! Find a selection of music to suit your taste and the tasks you perform and use this to cancel out all but the noisiest of situations.

> **What actions do you need to take to improve the sounds in your office?**

- *Colour* – Colour can have a substantial impact on your moods and your energy levels. You will have your own colour preferences, but there is also a body of thought that shows how colour affects people. According to the colour experts, red means power and passion, blue means efficiency and productivity and white means organisation and cleanliness. You can introduce these and other colours into your office to make your office flows even more smoothly. You have already chosen colours for your recurring action, project and reference files. Now you might want to use this information when you consider the colours of other items in your office such as art, vases, furniture, and soft furnishings. Go to page 149 to review the meanings of various colours and then select those which most closely relate to your needs, décor and personal preference.

What colours do you want to use in your office?

- *Storage* – How you store your equipment, paperwork and office tools is critical to your success. We've already shown you many options for storing your paperwork. Let's have a look at storing other kinds of office items. The good news is that with a little imagination and a few adjustments you can configure your storage to best suit your needs.

- *Shelving* – You can make your shelving work harder for you by making it fully adjustable. Always ensure shelves are strong enough for what you are storing. Be careful and spread weight evenly along the shelf to avoid bowing. Shelves above head height should store lighter weight items while lower shelves should be used for heavier items.

- *Drawers* – Use drawer dividers to keep items together as drawers are opened and closed; otherwise the contents end up a big jumble and you can't find things easily.

- *Rods and hooks* – These are perfect for hanging items on walls and on the backs of doors.
- *Boxes* – Their portability and flexibility makes them fantastic storage for stationery, cords and cables, CDs and DVDs. Magazine boxes are particularly useful for keeping things vertical and upright, making every item easy to access.

> **!** How many and what type of shelves, drawers, rods and hooks, boxes and folders do you need?

Step 2: Let's get functional!

Functional elements are things that make work easier. Let's take a closer look at some everyday organisational tools for your office flow and golden rules for using them. Simple labelling, checklists and procedures, as well as a variety of smart tools all come together to simplify your life. Spend a few moments setting up the following tools to save enormous amounts of time every day.

Notebook

Everyone needs to have a notebook to jot down the important information that comes their way in the course of each day. Here's how to create Notebook Flow:

- *Choose a notebook to suit your needs.* There are many different types, each with its advantages and disadvantages. For example, spiral and loose-leaf notebooks allow for lots of flexibility, while bound notebooks are more restrictive for everyday notes but great for journals, ideas books or dedicated topics, like renovations. You can even create a notebook on your computer to make notes as the day progresses.

- *Set up your note book.* Finding your way around your notebook can be a hassle. One terrific idea is to use sticky notes or removable tabs, which can be moved around as required. You might have a tab for meetings, one for messages and one for ideas. As you tear pages out of the notebook, you can move the tabs into a new position. If you have a loose-leaf notebook you can use tabbed dividers to create separate sections. You could have calls to make, contacts to update, client notes, websites to look up and project tabs. You then collect notes in each relevant section as information comes in. Many people prefer to simply record information as it comes in without creating any additional sections. Whatever your preference, a dedicated notebook is still an essential functional tool for everybody!

- *Taking notes.* When using your notebook, start by dating each entry. This gives you a sense of time and context, which is otherwise lost as time passes. Use a date stamp or hand write the date every time you write a new note. Then whenever you need to write something down, write it on the front side of the right hand page only. This makes it easy for you to tear out the page or a part of a page without having unrelated information on the reverse side. Using notebooks with recycled paper ensures this handy time saving approach is also easy on the environment. Then when you get to the end of the notebook you can turn it upside down and begin to write on the reverse side.

- *Dealing with your notes.* You now have two choices when dealing with the notes you have made in your notebook. You can either leave the notes in the book and action them one at a time or you can remove some or all entries and move them through your *Paper Flow* system. For example, if you wrote down a new address for a friend, you could enter the address straight from the notebook into your address book, or you could tear out the address and place it into your 'Contacts to Enter' recurring action file to be actioned later. The same thing applies to every other note you have taken, either action it directly from the notebook or move it through your *Paper Flow* system by moving it into your in-tray, recurring action files, project files or reference files depending on its nature and how busy you are at the time.

Tips for managing multiple note books ✓

The golden rule for notebooks is less is best – if you can get by with having just one, great. If you prefer to have a few notebooks around the home and office, then you need to assign each notebook to a certain location and then keep it there. You might have one in the office by the phone. Make sure it stays there, or at least always returns there by writing 'Office Notebook' on the front of it. If you are the sort of person who wakes up in the middle of the night with a brilliant idea, then you can have a 'Bedroom Notebook' that remains on your bedside table. Everyone seems to need one in the kitchen, so call it the 'Kitchen Notebook' and keep it in a magazine box by the phone in the kitchen.

! **Now decide how many notebooks you need, what type and size they need to be, then label them and place them in position ready to use from now on.**

Phone

How well is your phone working for you? Follow these steps to get *Phone Flow*:

- *Review the features.* Does your existing phone have all the features you need, for example, message bank, call forwarding, three-way chat, loud speaker, headset? Conversely, are your paying for features that you don't use or need? Now may also be a good time to review your current plan and ensure it's the best deal for the way you're using your phone. Consider what you have, what you need and how best to use your phone's features and plan to your advantage.

- *Storing numbers.* Many people keep all of their phone numbers in their phone which is very handy. Keep a hard copy or a back up of your numbers in case your phone is lost or stolen. Keep a list of regularly called numbers in your ready reference file and keep other numbers in your computer's 'contact list' or in your address book. Decide which numbers should be on speed dial and set them up.

- When making and receiving phone calls, use your notebook to capture notes as required. Similarly, when you play back your voice messages, record the date, time, caller and summary of the message in your notebook. This saves losing valuable information written on random scraps of paper. Remember some message bank services don't keep your messages longer than a few days so you can lose them. Action the messages directly from the notebook or tear them out and move them through *Paper Flow*.

- When you're out and about, divert calls from your home or office to your mobile phone so you can answer calls promptly.

Diary

Your diary is your personal record of future and past commitments, obligations and events.

- The golden rule for diaries is only use one diary. End of story.

- Choose either a digital or paper diary based on what works for you.

- Use your diary for everything. Put in anything that's going to take up your time so that you don't over commit yourself and end up being rushed and frazzled. Remember to allocate time for transferring between appointments, preparation and planning time and be sure to slot in time for regular breaks.

- Insert all your scheduled recurring action and project times into your diary. It's often the appointments with ourselves that we seem to put off. Make a habit of not letting things get in the way of your personal working and planning time.

- By keeping your master weekly schedule at the front of your diary you can enter these items on a weekly basis, fitting items around your other appointments and activities. For example, you may pay your bills on Mondays and you may do it at 9 am one week and at 2 pm the next week, depending on your other commitments in those weeks. Being firm but flexible is the key to ensuring you complete your weekly scheduled tasks along with everything else you need to do.

- Keep your diary with you at all times so you can check your availability before committing to requests or invitations.

Family calendar and household schedule

Your family calendar is your one-stop family guide to everyone's activities and whereabouts and is your key to life functioning smoothly.

- While your personal diary represents the detail of your daily activities, the family calendar captures basic information of who is coming and going, and who's meant to be where and when.

- Ideally have a column for each family member and capture the least amount of detail required for each entry. For example, if Ben has a dentist appointment, simply enter 'Ben – Dentist' and write in or block out the appointment time. Also use your family calendar to keep track of any babysitter bookings you may need to make by marking each entry with a 'B' or highlighter to ensure you're not left without a sitter.

- Let your household members know about the calendar's importance and make sure it's kept up to date. Double-booking is embarrassing and can be costly. Keep the family calendar in a central place for all to use, whether that be a wall in the kitchen or on the back of the pantry door.

- Your family schedule lists all household jobs including *Paper Flow* tasks. Keep this in a visible space so everyone knows when all the regular household activities are being undertaken.

Wednesday	Check and Process Claims to Make Empty In-Tray Check Correspondence Empty Filing Take reading to Café and have lunch with friends afterwards
Thursday	Empty In-Tray Check Correspondence Empty Filing Spend 1 hour working on Projects
Friday	Empty In-Tray Check Correspondence Empty Filing Spend 1 hour working on Projects
Saturday	Play Tennis
Sunday	Have Fun with Friends and Family

Party

Have your schedule close at hand

ⓔ Setting up computer files

Setting up your computer files to work with your *Paper Flow* system will really ensure you are on top of all information that comes your way. This means that you can simply mirror everything you have done in this *Paper Flow* book on your soft copy filing system on your computer. Typically, the two areas you'll be working with are within the My Documents folder of your office software and the In Box of your e-mail software. Then it's simply a matter of setting up folders for your Recurring Action, Project, Reference and Archive files within those two areas.

- Keep a ready-reference folder on your computer desktop for items you access frequently. Keep a list of all software serial numbers as well as Usernames and Passwords for email accounts and subscriptions or sign-ups.

- Use a password to protect files containing important information to restrict unauthorised users.

- Keep your computer desktop clutter-free. Unless it's a shortcut to a file or program you use daily, remove all icons from your desktop. So you don't lose anything, create a folder called 'unused desktop icons' and drop them in there.

- Schedule time to complete your computer tasks. In the case of Recurring Action items, this is best done at the same time you are doing your paper-based tasks. For example, when you're handling your paper based correspondence, also handle any outstanding correspondence in your e-mail in box. For projects, you will naturally do the same.

Back up, back up, back up! Without routinely backing up your files you risk losing important information in the event of theft, fire, flood or malfunction. Decide how often you're going to back up and then schedule times into your diary so you don't forget. Weekly is often enough for most people, but you may need to do it more or less frequently depending on what you store on your computer. Store your back-ups off-site, where possible, or at the very least away from your computer. There are secure websites that will routinely back up your computer's data. When deciding on where to store your back-up files choose the most secure and trusted source available.

> **How often will you back up your files?**

Turn *Paper Flow* into eFlow by rearranging your computer files in a simple folder structure that mirrors your *Paper Flow* system. Here are some examples shown in 'My Documents' and 'Microsoft Outlook'. Numbering your folder names will keep them in priority order.

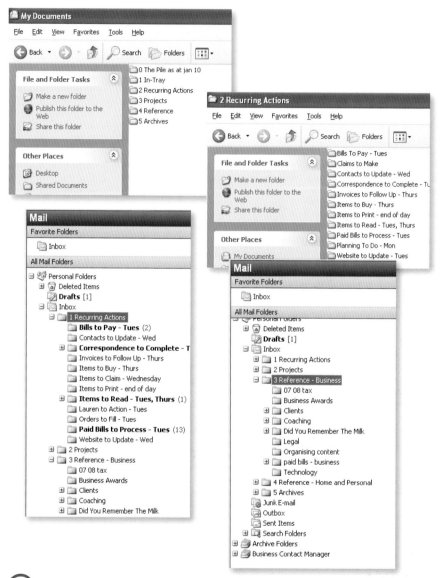

Tips for mastering email

Don't be a slave to your e-mail. Scheduling regular e-mail times throughout the day will ensure you don't fall into the trap of responding to every e-mail as soon as it arrives, which may not be a good use of your time. You should control your e-mails rather than having them control you.

Stationery

Your stationery needs to be ready for action whenever you are.

Don't turn your work space into a branch office of your favourite stationery store. Just keep the essentials at hand and extra supplies can go elsewhere. The key to an effective stationery supply is having the right amount on stand-by, having the right amount in reserve and having everything in good working order. There is nothing worse than grabbing a pen only to find it doesn't work or using a stapler that jams all the time. You will need good quality, fully operational stationery, including:

- letter opener
- writing paper
- envelopes
- stamps
- greeting and gift cards
- sticky notes
- date stamp
- stapler and staples
- hole puncher (with a guide)
- pens, pencils, highlighters, markers
- erasers
- pencil sharpener
- label maker
- scissors
- adhesive tape
- glue stick
- ruler
- calculator

Having some or all of these items in a box or on a tray turns your stationery supply into a portable 'toolbox' ready to work for you wherever you are.

Resource box

A resource box holds items you use on a daily basis. Its contents could include 'to do' lists, shopping lists, your notebook and your ready-reference file. Place these items close at hand at your workstation. Keep these items in a magazine box so they are vertical and easily accessible. Your resource box will save your life more than once a day!

Notice board

Notice boards are great functional tools for holding invitations, postcards, photos and important information. You can use cork boards, chalk boards, white boards or magnetic boards, the choice is yours. But make sure the information stays current, otherwise the items on your board become just another pile. Many people use the fridge or the inside of a cupboard for their notice boards. Remember, some people in your household or office may not notice the notice board! If there's something you need them to know, make sure you direct them to the notice board. A great alternative to a notice board is a 'Notice Book'. Simply place any item that would normally go onto a noticeboard into a display book, label it 'Notice Book' and place it in your resource box. Many people live without a notice board altogether and simply process all their paper through their regular *Paper Flow* system.

Step 4: Let's get emotional!

The emotional elements of your workspace are all those things that trigger your senses. To make sure your space really feels right and works for you, ask yourself, "What do I want to see, hear, feel and smell in my workspace?" Photos, music, flowers, plants, fruit, snacks, scented candles and art are just some of the ingredients you can play around with to make your workspace great. Robert placed his golf trophy and a few family holidaying photos on his office shelf. These symbolise the balance he needs between work and play.

Dirty ashtrays, wilted plants, dusty ornaments, out-dated information and old equipment all have a negative effect on your emotions. Susan removed her collection of snow globes that were cluttering up her workstation and she finally got rid of her old computer gathering dust in the corner. She hung her university certificate on the wall above her desk as a reminder of her achievement and hung some of her favourite art pieces on the wall to inspire her. She couldn't believe how much these simple changes could lift her emotions. She finally felt comfortable and at ease.

You want enough personality in your office that it reflects who you are, but not so much personality that it is cluttered and distracting. Balance is the key.

> **!** **Which personal touches will you add to bring your work space to life?**

You've made it!

Congratulations on reaching your milestone!

Now that the physical, functional and emotional elements of your workspace are working in harmony, you have achieved *Office Flow*. Your *Paper Flow* system is now working in the perfect environment. *Paper Flow* will serve you faithfully every day of every week, of every year. In only a few minutes each day you will process paper coming in, through and out of your office, simply and easily. You will wonder how you ever lived without it and you will never have to live without it again, ever!

Ode to *Paper Flow*

You'll find what you want when you need it

If your desk is clear every day

When messy piles become organised files

Your paper work is now paper play

We've taught you just what you needed

We've given as much as we know

With the aid of all our instructions

You can now make your own *Paper Flow*

You're cruising

Let's look at your results for this chapter. You have:

- ☐ reviewed the physical elements of your paper storage and processing areas of your home and office

- ☐ reviewed the functional elements of your office and created checklists, guidelines and rules to make your office function smoothly

- ☐ reviewed the emotional elements of your office and added or removed items to create a space that emotionally supports you

It's FLOW time!!

> One who asks a question is a fool for
> five minutes; one who does not ask a
> question remains a fool forever.
>
> *Chinese Proverb*

Frequently asked questions

Paper Flow has introduced you to a new way of thinking with new habits to adopt. Allow yourself time to put it in place and then it will become harder not to do it than to do it! Along your journey, questions may crop up from time to time. Below are answers to some anticipated questions.

My in-tray is turning into a paper pile and I just can't face it! What should I do?

An in-tray pile is just a symptom of office constipation – the paper is flowing in but it isn't flowing out! Remember when we said that the frequency of emptying your in-tray depended on the volume of paper coming in? If it is piling up too quickly, you simply need to empty it more frequently. So, instead of once a week, make it twice a week, or more often if necessary. In the meantime, get back on track by tackling your constipated in-tray like this:

- Pour a drink, put on some music and get your date stamp, stapler, pen and hole puncher ready for attack. Count the items in the in-tray and write it down.

- get a timer out and set it for eight minutes
- ready, set, go! Now tackle the in-tray one piece at a time, starting at the top. Remember that paper can never go back – it's on a one-way trip out!
- open, date stamp and staple where needed. Now ask it: Do I have to do something with you – yes or no?
- a 'yes' takes it to your action station – place it into the appropriate action file
- a 'no' sends it to your Items to File folder or the bin
- now, repeat this process for every item at record speed until the timer goes off
- phew! How many pieces of paper did you move? Write it down. Now you have a personal best! Set the timer again and see if you can beat your own personal best
- when you have finished, go to Items to File and file them. Come on, it's that easy and it's that hard, but it has to be done!

The eight-minute power burst can work to break the procrastination pattern. Use it any time you become overwhelmed by a task. Try just eight minutes at a time and be amazed at how much you can get done. Use eight minute power bursts to whittle down your emails as well. What else can you apply eight-minute power bursts to?

My paper hits the in-tray but the rest of the family has paper all over the place and I just can't get them to co-operate.

Hmmm, when we get all fired up about something we automatically expect everyone else to fall into line with our latest, greatest idea. When we want to get fit, we want everyone to come on our walks with us; when we get excited about a great film, we expect everyone else to love it too. But they don't want to get fit and they don't like the film and we get upset and take it personally. Well it's not personal and it's perfectly normal. Everyone is at different points in their lives, and while getting organised is your number one priority at the moment, it's just not everyone's priority right now. So, that explains the problem, but what can you do about it? How about just deciding that being organised is your personal goal and you want it for selfish reasons – you want more free time and a sense of control. In order to do this you need the paperwork of the entire household or things won't happen. You have three choices:

1   You can extract and gather the paper from other household members and take control of all paper, accepting that their lack of co-operation isn't a personal attack. You need to do this with joy and see it as a gift you are giving to them – that is, the gift of organised paper. The key is not to do it with resentment or hostility, and above all don't be a martyr! Get over it and just gather up the paper with a smile and let the *Paper Flow*. Your attitude and lack of nagging will totally flabbergast your family and they will be hanging out waiting for the 'spell' you are under to break. But the spell won't break because you are getting what you want – the paper into the in-tray, control of the paperwork and the ultimate in *Paper Flow*.

2   You can simply refuse to process any paper that doesn't hit the in-tray. Let the family know you are on a 'paper strike' for anything that doesn't enter the in-tray and they will suffer the consequences arising from that, whether they be missed appointments, late payment of bills or lost documents. This is a more aggressive approach and often works well. To make this work, you must let it play out and let the consequences hit them and, unfortunately, maybe you too!

3   You can use the usual arsenal of tactics: bribery, corruption, crying, throwing a tantrum, withholding services, sulking or nagging.

I am great at paying my bills, but I just hate filing them. What can I do?

Filing is a key component of *Paper Flow* and to block the flow here means it is beginning to form the dreaded paper dam. Although we know that avoiding filing now means much more work later on, we still do it and then we go into a spin about the inevitable filing backlog.

The simple and universal cure to the 'I hate filing' excuse is simply to ask: Which is worse – filing four pieces of paper a day or having to tackle piles of unfiled stuff? Obviously, the answer is tackling the pile of unfiled stuff! We suggest you bypass the 'Items to File' folder altogether and simply place items directly into their appropriate reference files as soon as they are actioned.

I don't have time to process my paperwork, so it just piles up everywhere! How do I make time?

When we don't have time for something, it means we do have time for something else. What are the things you are making time for and actually doing? *Paper Flow* is a time and mind liberator, not a time-taker. It only takes your time when it is neglected and left to fester and grow into piles. Paper will never take less time than when it is fresh and new. As it ages in a pile its time requirement grows, along with the size of the pile. Doing it now will save time and money in the future. Think about ways you can fit a little extra *Paper Flow* time into your day – get up a few minutes earlier, go to bed a little later, play with your paper during your favourite TV show or take stuff to work and do it in your breaks. Imagine how liberated you will feel once that paper pile is gone.

I have trouble deciding on how long to keep things and am afraid to let my paperwork go. What should I do?

Fear of letting go of paper, just in case you might need it one day, is a common fear and everyone has their own level of anxiety about paper's final destination – the recycling bin. Once it's gone, it's gone and we fear that the 'Paper Police' will knock on our door and demand a bank statement from the distant past. Let us reassure you, the 'Paper Police' are as realistic as the 'Fashion Police' – a good idea, but non-existent. Paper is meant to serve and support us, not enslave us.

Most paper visits us for a short time only and is happy to leave once it has served its purpose. By holding on to it for longer than necessary it smothers our active paper and crowds up our system. Go back to every category of paper you keep and review the limits you have set for each of them. For example, when keeping bank statements, how many do you want to have in your reference files and how many do you need in archives? Once you set the limit, stick to it and let paper flow out of your system just as easily as it flows in.

Double check with your legal or financial advisor on the required times for keeping important documents, then release your paper once and for all.

I start doing my paperwork but I soon get distracted. How can I stay on track and get the job done?

This one is easy to solve, but be advised – it involves handcuffs or some other restraining devices! When we are trying to stay focused but continually get distracted, we need to use some strong tactics. Why not try "locking" yourself in? You cannot be released until the job is done. So pay all the bills and then release yourself; make all the calls and then release yourself; work on your project and then release yourself. This will stop you leaving the space and will keep you focused on the job. If your organising requires movement, place a chair in the doorway of the room you are working in. Place a box on the chair for anything that has to leave the room. If distractions come from other people, go to another room or place a sign on your back saying 'Please do not disturb'. Try closing the door. Definitely turn off emails and let phone calls go to message bank. Put on some music and continue until the CD is finished. Set a timer and work until the bell dings. Set yourself a reward, for example, when you are done you can have a coffee and a muffin – but not before.

I am so sick of paper! How can I go paperless?

While going paperless is a great idea, nobody can ever be truly paperless. There are always going to be documents you will keep in hard copy for official or sentimental reasons. However, you can reduce the volume of paper coming into your in-tray. Try each of the following and see how you go:

- Pay bills on time (direct debit where possible) to stop reminders coming in.
- Receive bills electronically and file on the computer.
- Download statements (bank, frequent flyer, loans etc.) monthly and save them in your relevant computer reference file.
- Place a 'no junk mail' sign on your letterbox.
- Stop collecting paper throughout the day. For example, instead of picking up a brochure, note the website in your notebook and look it up when you return home.
- Contact companies that usually send you paper and request electronic correspondence instead.
- Print off as little as possible.

What if I don't have any space to put things?

From our experience it's never about the space, it's always about the stuff. We all have to adapt to our space, large or small. The fact is we will simply fill the space we have available. Your entire *Paper Flow* system only needs to take up the equivalent of half a bookcase. Your piles probably take up more than that right now. If space is a real issue, then you have to keep less. There is no other way to go – you either get more space or have less stuff! Set very strict limits on what you keep and stick to your limits.

What can I do about all the piles that have accumulated all over the house, especially along the hallway? We look as though we are moving in or out, but the sad truth is we have lived here for ten years.

You may need to engage in the great sport of 'tossing'! The first thing to do is to box up your piles so they look like neatly packed items. You could use champagne boxes from your local liquor store to house your piles temporarily until they are whittled away when you play the Great Australian Toss (rules below).

- Pick a number between 20 and 40. This is now known as your tosser number. For the purposes of this exercise we will nominate 32.

- Now, every day you must toss 32 pieces of paper away.

- So, open a box of your 'French champagne' and remove the first 32 pieces of paper from the box.

- Now, process these papers into your system and count the number of items that get tossed (with the aim of tossing 32).

- You may need to extract more paper from your boxes because some pieces will be kept and you must actually toss 32 pieces before you finish for that day.

- Once you reach 32, you can exit the field of play with pride and a firm resolve to play again tomorrow.

- Okay. So you didn't win an impressive silver-plated trophy, but you are starting to win the war you have declared on your 'toss-able' paper, and that has to be better than a dust-gathering trophy.

Congratulations! You're now a Great Australian Tosser!

My paperwork is really functioning well but I have so much stationery. How do I manage all my pens and gadgets?

Life is all about limits – we have credit limits, weight limits, speed limits, alcohol limits. The list of limits is limitless. So let's limit our stationery. Try these ideas and see what works for you:

- Go to your stationery drawer and desktop and gather up a handful of pens.

- Throw out the ones that don't work and place a rubber band around the rest of them.

- Repeat until all the pens are rubber-banded together in little bundles.
- Pick out a selection of your favourites – the ones you want to use and the ones you like best.
- Place them into a suitable cup, glass or container on your desk.
- Place the rest in a box and label it 'Writing Implements'.
- Repeat this process for your pencils, markers, highlighters etc.
- Keep a few on the desk and the rest in the box. Place the box up high on a shelf.

Whenever you need a new pen go to your box and pick one more, making sure you have thrown the old one out. Do not purchase a new pen until all the ones in the box are gone.

Now all you need to do is repeat the process for every other gadget you have collected. You only need one stapler, one hole puncher, one date stamp and so on per workstation or one set overall if your collection of tools is in a portable container.

I love all of my recurring action files but I find that, while I have set a day, I am not always in the right frame of mind to process them. What should I do?

Schedule tasks around the times you feel up and the times you feel less than up. Stuart used to struggle with completing tasks after lunch because he felt tired and unfocused. Once he understood that he could work with his own internal energy levels, rather than against them, things really started to flow for him. He decided on a short walk after lunch to take in some fresh air and to clear his head. Stuart then planned to do recurring action items (low-level activities) when he was in 'off-peak' time. Simply doing a few short bursts of routine tasks kept him going and once they were done the energy returned. He even said he felt that a big load was lifted when he realised that he no longer needed to force himself to concentrate. He now uses his pre-lunch periods for all his high-level thinking and tasks.

Using your peak and off-peak time wisely is only one way to enhance your *Paper Flow*. Did you know that taking breaks actually improves performance? Short power-naps can work wonders; a 15-minute meditation can calm a hectic day and even swapping between tasks can energise you. Don't feel guilty about taking these breaks, because your subconscious is still working on the solutions to your problems, and the answers often flow when your mind is relaxed and still.

One of the best things you can do to make your paper really flow is to review your past week and plan your future week. Look for what worked and what didn't to help plan the week ahead.

After I set up my project files, I realised that I have too many projects, but I can't decide which ones to cull. What should I do?

A lot of the success in managing your paperwork comes down to time management. If you've only got ten hours a week to work on your projects then that's all the time you've got. It's as simple as that. Often we take on more than we can manage because we haven't done the simple math. The old adage applies here that the fastest way to do many things is to do one thing at a time. Juggling ten projects at a time in this case would mean you have on average less than one hour a week to work on each one. Remember the old adage that the greatest way to do many things is to do one thing at a time. Prioritise your projects – which are the most important?

Where should I file the notes that I take about my *Paper Flow* system, so I remember all the decisions I made while working through this book?

Setting up *Paper Flow* is a one-off activity. It has a beginning, a middle in which you must make some decisions and set up your system, and an end. If this is sounding vaguely like a project to you, that would be correct! So treat it like your other projects. Make time for it in your diary, set up a project file in which you can keep your notes as you're working through the project and set a target date for its completion. At the end, some of your notes will become reference material. For example, you will keep a master list of all your files and the rules of how much of each subject matter to keep and for how long. You might file that list in a display book called 'My Filing System', or 'Paper Flow' or simply place it in your Ready Reference file – whatever works for you!

How long will this system take to set up?

Setting up your in-tray takes a few seconds using a temporary container, or as long as it takes to get to the nearest office supply store, if you don't already own a suitable container. A recurring action file takes two minutes to set up. Setting up each project file takes two minutes and filling in your project planning sheet takes another five minutes. Each reference binder takes about fifteen minutes to set up – writing the index page and typing out the labels for the tabs on your label machine, and hole-punching and inserting your pages. So the average household can have a complete system up and running in a day or so. This doesn't include going back over all the old piles and sorting them and bringing them into your new system. You can tackle that over a few weeks by doing half an hour a day, or you might want to nail it over a day or two. It's completely up to you. The point is, this is really easy to set up and it will last forever.

My home office is upstairs and my front door is downstairs. I keep forgetting to take the things I need with me in the morning. What can I do to save me running up and down the stairs all day filling an out-bag hanging on the front door?

All you need is a 'Leaving the House' or 'Leaving the Office' checklist. This is a simple list stuck to the back of the door or a list that is framed and hung next to the door which serves as a daily reminder of what to take with you when you're leaving the house or office. Anyone who is the least bit forgetful will appreciate this one. If you're worried about how it will look, rest assured, your friends and colleagues will be impressed with your level of organisation and will no doubt copy this approach.

I've got to arrange a weekend away in a month's time. It's not a big project, so I don't want to waste time setting up a dedicated file, but it's also not a recurring action, so where do I park my stuff until it all gets done?

Why not set up a travel project file to be used for any travel or weekends away you have in the future. By not dedicating a file to each specific trip, you save time and energy. The file will either be active or dormant. You cannot escape the fact that each trip is a project but some projects do repeat. Parties are another example of projects that repeat over time.

I'm constantly coming home with my wallet full of little receipts. Some are for tax, some are for purchases, some I don't need and they make me dizzy. How do I deal with them all quickly?

When you get home from work or the shops, or the weekend away, open your wallet (where these receipts are usually kept) and take them all out and dump them straight into your in-tray. When you empty your in-tray, you are going to file them as follows. Any business related expenses go into your 'Items to Process' file, for recording in your financial software package or in your Claims to Make file to be claimed through work. Then they will be put into an envelope with the month on it and 'Business' and put into a storage box marked 'Receipts'. Any receipts for items that come with a warranty, like the refrigerator or the kettle, can be stapled to the back of the warranty and filed in the Warranties and Manuals file! Other items like receipts for clothing and gifts can be placed in the receipts box in envelopes marked with the month and year and labelled general shopping receipts. Simple! Refer to our advice for handling small receipts on page 88.

With three children at school, I am constantly getting forms that need to be filled out, but I can't do them immediately. Where do I keep them so that they get done and get to the right person on time?

These forms are simply Correpondence to Complete items. In order to return completed forms on time, you may need to increase the frequency of dealing with this file to once every two or three days.

My child brings home volumes of artwork, including these amazing 'super structures' made of cardboard, paper and paint. I feel so guilty about throwing them out, but we are swamped with them. How do I prevent the house from getting taken over?

A memory box for each child is an essential item in your *Paper Flow* system. Use a large storage box, A3 size is perfect, and fill it to your heart's' content. Once a year go through the box and cull items back to a reasonably-sized collection. For large structures and physical projects, take photographs of your child with the project to have a lasting memory and you can discard the project after an appropriate period of 'display time'. You may want to set up a dedicated spot where the 3D art gets 'displayed' and when that place (shelf or wall) is filled, then it's the 'one in, one out' rule. A3 display folders or art folios are perfect for holding the current year's paintings and drawings. Create a visual display by hanging some picture frames in a designated spot and rotate the art on a regular basis.

Appendix 1

Example *Paper Flow* Schedule

Action:	Mon	Tues	Wed	Thurs	Fri	Sat	Sun
Empty In-tray		X		X		X	
Pay Bills		X					
Update Contacts			X				
Process Claims					X		
File Items	X		X		X		
Process Correspondence	X	X	X	X	X	X	X
Review Reading						X	
Work on Projects	X		X		X		

Appendix 2

Meanings of Colours

Up until now you have probably selected colours of items based on your personal preferences. You either liked a colour or you didn't. You preferred one colour over another. Your choice of colours was influenced by your preferences, your décor and what was available. But colours have meanings and each colour has its very own personality! By knowing a little about the meanings of each colour you will be able to choose colours of items in your office that will actually help you with the task at hand and you may gain huge benefits in managing your *Paper Flow*.

Colour is a form of non-verbal communication. Every time you see a colour you actually have a physical and emotional reaction to it. Most of this occurs at a subconscious level so you are often not aware of your reactions on a moment to moment basis. Your *Paper Flow* system involves the selection of a whole range of tools: binders, storage boxes, folders, diaries, notebooks and even your stapler, hole punch and tape dispenser. The colours of these may have an impact on how you feel when using these items and will ultimately affect your productivity. Read on to learn the meanings of some common colours and use this information when making your colour selections.

Blue is the colour of communication and productivity. It also represents trust, loyalty, creativity, intelligence, peace, clarity, order and wisdom. Blue is very calming and relaxes our nervous system. People retain more information written in blue and are more productive when they have blue in their surroundings. So why not use blue pens, blue highlighters and have some blue in your workspace. It could be as simple as a touch of blue in some artwork, soft furnishings or rugs.

Green is a restful colour and it abounds in nature. It also represents peace, harmony, health, growth and the environment. Surgeons used to wear hospital greens and TV stations have green rooms. Both have the intention of calming people. If you need a little calm in your life, introduce some green into your office.

Red is the colour of fire, blood, enthusiasm, action, passion and energy and gives us a sense of protection from anxiety and fear. People feel powerful and confident when driving red cars or carrying or wearing red items. Red is good for giving shy people courage. Many public speakers use red to add to their credibility and confidence. If you need a little confidence boost simply add some red to your life.

Pink is all about sugar and spice and all things nice. It represents calmness, romance, love and friendship. It is a great colour to reduce anger. It is hard to be angry at pink. Use pink if you need to calm someone. It's a great colour to have in the complaints department.

Yellow is a happy colour full of joy and good cheer. It is associated with intellect and energy. Yellow is fun so splash it around to add a little fun into your space. Yellow encourages communication and sparks creativity. Yellow is a good colour to have when brainstorming.

Orange combines the energy of red and the happiness of yellow. It represents determination, attraction, success, encouragement and stimulation.

Purple is the colour of royalty, power, nobility. luxury and ambition. It conveys wealth and extravagance. If you want wisdom, independence, creativity, mystery and magic in your life, purple is the colour for you.

White is all about goodness, innocence, purity and perfection. White symbolizes new beginnings as well as being the colour of organisation. If you need to fake it until you make it in the area of office organisation, white may be the way to go.

Black is elegant, formal and a little mysterious. It indicates understated power and confidence. It is conservative and sophisticated.

Brown and Beige are stable, reliable and approachable. They are great colours to tone things down a little because they are conservative and relaxing. Brown gives the sense of wholesomeness and being environmentally friendly.

Grey is timeless, solid and conservative. It is said that grey goes with everything. It can also be formal and sophisticated. Grey is a safe colour and silver-grey is often used for computer components, office equipment and accessories.

Appendix 3

What should I keep?

Some documents should be kept indefinitely. They include:

- important documents including such items as birth and marriage certificates, court orders, wills and passports (these are listed on page 61)

- medical history records, which can just be a summary of conditions, operations, reports and injuries

- employment and educational records, which should be kept for proof of experience and expertise

Tax legislation determines a lot of what we need to keep. Always check tax implications before disposing of any financial records.

In Australia, tax information needs to be kept for the five years prior to receiving your latest assessment notice. Each country has its own rules, so check with your tax agent. You need to keep anything that was included in your tax return in case of audit. So hang on to evidence of all income declared and all deductions and rebates claimed.

Some documents should be kept for the life of the business/investment/asset/product/liability plus around five to seven years afterwards. These include:
- share and investment information
- business records
- pension and superannuation information
- rental property records
- vehicle ownership
- insurance policies
- mortgages
- loans and leases

- major purchases
- warranties and instructions
- major repairs
- improvements and renovations
- rental agreements and payments

Most other receipts and records come down to personal choice. Keep these non-tax related items for one to five years or so depending on your comfort level.

These include:
- utility bills
- bank and credit card statements
- membership and subscription renewals
- medical receipts
- store purchase receipts
- old diaries and calendars

Everyone's circumstances are different, so use these simple guidelines as a starting point and get professional advice to ensure you comply with all your legal and financial obligations.

Appendix 4

Example Templates for the Front of Reference Files

cars

VICROADS Registration Honda Jazz
Acc No: 3366 9988 Due: 16 March

AAMI Insurance Honda Jazz
Policy No: 2312 4578 Due: 27 June

Service and Repairs Honda Jazz
Mechanic: Rob Williams 999 8888

VICROADS Registration Holden SS Commodore
Acc No: 6633 8899 Due: 7 September

AAMI Insurance Holden SS Commodore
Policy No: 4578 2312 Due: 4 July

Service and Repairs Holden SS Commodore
All Star Motors: 8888 9999

Breeze Road Tolls
Acc No: 8521 3258 Due: 28 May
Direct Debit from Savings Account

Drivers' Licences
Mary Licence No: 123698 Fred Licence No: 896321

Fines and Demerits
Parking, Speeding, Driving Fines and Demerits

Appendix
Vehicle Purchase Documents, Old Insurance Claims

www.paperflow.com.au

investments

Stock Broker Information and Statements
Malcolm Prior: 5698 2541 HIN No: 124 5678 Password: bull

BHP Mining Shares
Dividends Dec & June

ANZ Bank Shares
Dividends April

Telstra Shares
Dividends May & November

Investment Portfolio
Portfolio of all share holdings

Tax
Receipts for tax
NOTE: small tax receipts in envelope in receipts box

Shares – Purchase Statements
5000 shares purchased on 20 June 2006

Globe Superannuation
Member No: 5566 8832
Phone No: 5623 8956
Web: www.globesuper.com.au   Password: Super

Always Superannuation
Member No: 8832 5566
Phone No: 8956 5623
Web: www.alwayssuper.com.au   Password: retire

Appendix
Superannuation Booklet, Banking Terms & Conditions

www.paperflow.com.au

utilities

AGL Gas

Account No: 5432 1234
Phone No: 9632 1478
Accounts Due: Jan, April, July, Oct

Origin Electricity

Account No: 5432 1235
Phone No: 9632 1479
Accounts Due: Feb, May, Aug, Nov

Melbourne Council Rates

Account No: 6666 8888
Phone No: 2583 6921
Accounts Due: September

Yarra Valley Water

Account No: 753 951
Phone No: 2356 8987
Accounts Due: March, June, Sept, Dec

AAMI Insurance – Home and Contents

Policy No: 8945 23
Phone No: 3568 8451
Policy Expires: 11 August

Bigpond Internet

Account No: 3692 8741 3698 Password: riley
Phone No: 7894 5612
Accounts Due: 10th of the Month

Optus Phone

Account No: 753 951 Password: anderson
Phone No: 2356 8987
Accounts Due: 16th of the Month

3 Mobile Phone

Account No: 3697 4512 Password: bella
Phone No: 6391 7845
Accounts Due: 25th of the Month Plan Expires: 25th August

Foxtel Pay TV

Account No: 3654 219 Password: griffin
Phone No: 5689 5421
Accounts Due: 4th of the Month

Appendix

Booklets relating to utility accounts

www.paperflow.com.au

Gallery of Tools

Here are all the tools we have referred to regularly throughout *Paper Flow*. Use this list to help you decide which tools and containers you need to complete your system.

in-tray with date stamp and timer on stand by

desk top file box with suspension files and manila folders

daily tools in box rather than drawer make them portable

drop down file makes a great out-bag

step file with manila folders holding recurring action and project files

clear file box with display book and plastic pockets

Gallery of Tools

lever arch folders used as
reference files

contents sheet for reference binder
with tabs lined up

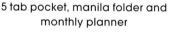

5 tab pocket, manila folder and
monthly planner

display book with clear cover

magazine boxes with display books,
notebooks and diary

magazine box with gusseted plastic
pockets

Gallery of Tools

filing drawer with suspension files and manila folders

portable file with suspension files and manila folders

assorted storage boxes

A3 boxes used for archives

notice board holding weekly planner

archive box with box file inserts

Thanks to kikki.K for these images of stationery items and tools.
To find your nearest store visit **www.kikki-k.com.au**

Acknowledgements

Many people helped develop *Paper Flow* and we would like to particularly thank the following: Kristina Karlsson and the team at kikki.K for embracing *Paper Flow* workshops since 2002, Carla Fletcher and kikki.K for providing the gorgeous photography, workshop participants and private clients for giving valuable feedback over the years, Di Websdale-Morrissey and Rebecca Hill for early editorial and advice on finding a common voice and style, and Vikki Siliato, our designer, for an excellent job of turning slabs of text into a visual delight.

MaryAnne would also like to thank the following people for their love, support and input: my brothers Harry and Peter, my mother Helen, and to my late dad Wally, you would have been so proud! To my children David, Michelle and Amanda, their partners and my four little treasures Max, Mia, Harry and Keeley, you bring me continuous pride and joy. To my husband David, I love you and you are my rock. To my many friends and business associates, thank you for all your support and understanding. And finally to all my wonderful clients and workshop participants, thank you for sharing your challenges and for allowing me into a small part of your life.

Brigitte would like to especially thank the following people for their love, support, patience, generosity and humour which helped make *Paper Flow* possible: my husband Simon, Mary and Ted Johnson (Mum and Dad), Franny Johnson, Lauren Siliato and my beautiful children Grace, Lachlan and James. Thanks to my clients for sharing with me their challenges and goals and all the thousands of people who have embraced my first book *Did You Remember The Milk?* Also thanks to 'the girls' for being there through thick and thin and my uncle Seamus who helped me get 'the nerve' so I could finish it!

About in8 and the Paper Flow® System

in8 Pty Ltd is a professional organising business founded by MaryAnne Bennie. The Paper Flow® System was created and developed by MaryAnne and since 2002 thousands of people's lives have been transformed by Paper Flow.

While the book, *Paper Flow the ultimate guide to making paperwork easy* is filled with all the information you need to set up your very own Paper Flow system at home or at work, you may find that you prefer to have additional assistance with a more personal touch. A range of options is available to you:

- Certified Paper Flow Consultants are ready to save you time, money and stress. They will assist you to better manage your possessions, your information, your time and your space at home and at work by helping you install the Paper Flow System quickly and easily.

- Certified Paper Flow Presenters are ready to conduct workshops in an area near you and demonstrate step-by-step how to install Paper Flow in your home or office.

in8 specialises in developing systems around people. Personal values and identity are important and are respected and nurtured at all times. Paper Flow Consultants work together with you to build systems that get you up and running in the short term and evolve and change with you in the long term.

Paper Flow training is also available for corporations and small businesses and MaryAnne Bennie is a sought after speaker at Conferences and Seminars.

To find a consultant or an event near you please go to:
www.paperflow.com.au
www.in8.com.au

Fact: Two hours of every day are wasted due to disorganisation. Is this time you can really afford to be losing?

The most effective route to more time, money and success? Getting organised.

Let's face it – we could all do with a few more hours in the day. If we had just a little extra time, all the household repairs would be tackled, the kids' lunches would always be made the night before and those all-important work goals would already have been achieved. But what if it isn't about having more time – what if it's really about using the time you do have more effectively?

Organisation gives you power. It allows you to take control and start living life to the full, free from the stresses that come with 'never having the time' to focus on your business/read the children a bedtime story/take that holiday you've been dreaming of. And the best part about getting organised? **Absolutely anyone can do it!** But just as with most things in life, it's a lot easier with a little support...

Are You Milking It?

If you're really keen to take control of your time, your home, your money, your business and your life, then **Milking It: Systems for Success in Life, Business and Home** is here to help. Milking It is an online personal coaching program that you can take in the comfort and privacy of your own home or office.

Over 40 fun video tutorials will coach you through twelve different aspects of your life, while accompanying workbooks, bonus downloads, forums and interviews with expert guests will make sure you take action to move your life forward and stay on track. This powerful online coaching program is completely geared to busy mums.

Fast track your goals, dreams and plans TODAY – visit

www.areyoumilkingit.com

Did You Remember the Milk? is the ultimate home and life organising website helping thousands of busy people. The site is packed to the brim with practical, comprehensive tools to help you with every area of your life. Our popular organiser *Did You Remember The Milk?* is THE companion for busy households:

- No need to reinvent the wheel.

- The book, *Did You Remember The Milk?* comes in hard copy binder or 318 page e-book with fillable pages

- 14 different sections, from finances to food, laundry to luggage, grooming to garden

- Written by experienced life-coach and mumpreneur

Contained within the pages of **Did You Remember The Milk?** is thousands of dollars' worth of value and the ability to save you a truly incredible amount of time.

Don't just take our word for it – this indispensible guide has quite literally transformed the lives of thousands of people. Here's what others have been saying about their 'Milk?' experience:

"'Did You Remember The Milk?' has been **my saviour** in managing our busy family"

"LOVE your planner. Great for my crazy, busy, insane life. It's a **god send**"

"…the **best** thing I have ever seen in relation to organisation"

"…a fabulous book, helping to **lighten the load** of the busy working mother!"

"…it **"does all the thinking for me"** and is the "one stop shop" for all the most important information in our life."

"Thank you so much for your **life changing** book. I have so much **more time to enjoy life.**"

Make today the day you change your life:

www.didyouremberthemilk.com.au